MODELLING *the* BRITISH RAIL *Era*

A Modellers Guide
to the
Classic Diesel and Electric Age

by
Ian Fleming, Steve Flint, Ken Gibbons and Jeff Taylor

Booklaw Publications

SANTONA

Frontispiece

Front Cover. *Western class 52 No. 1049 draws into New Quay station with a through service train from Paddington. New Quay, built by Ken Gibbons, is one of our featured layouts and demonstates how long main line sized trains can be represented on minimum space layouts.*

Frontispiece. *Another scene on New Quay. Reminiscent perhaps of the last days of rail services in South West Wales. Hymek No. D7059, a detailed up Hornby model, heads for the milk factory siding at Felin Fach.*

Top right. *Speedlink traffic depicted in 1983 on Reighton with air braked VGA vans in their original condition.*

Centre right. *Shunting the old order. Class 25 No. 25044 shuffles traditional vacuum braked van traffic in the yard on Kyle of Tongue, an archetypal Scottish Highland railway terminus layout set in 1976.*

Bottom right. *The Hymek is seen shunting at New Quay with a solitary van for the local agricultural merchants association.*

MODELLING *the* BRITISH RAIL *Era*

CONTENTS

Modelling the British Rail Era.

First Published in 2001

British Library Cataloguing-in-Publication Data.
A catalogue record for this book is available from the British Library.
Copyright © 2001 by Ian Fleming, Steve Flint, Ken Gibbons, Jeff Taylor.

Printed by The Amadeus Press, West Yorkshire.

ISBN 0 9507960 8 5

Acknowledgements

The authors and publishers would like to thank the following individuals for their valued assistance in the preparation of this book. Nigel Bowyer, Greg Brooks, Mick Bryan, Ian S Carr, Colin Craig, Graham Gibbons, Jon Gregory, David Larkin, Dennis Lovatt, Ian Manderson, Pauline McKenna, Steve Moore, Mick Nicholson, Dr Michael Rhodes, Paul Shannon, Dave Skipsey, Brian Sunman, Phil Sutton, Steve Titheridge, Mike Turner, John Vaughan, Paul Wade, and Bob Wallace. We also acknowledge the cooperation of the publishers of Railway Modeller, British Railway Modelling and Rail Express magazines.

Wagon diagrams created on CAD by Colin Craig. Artwork, graphics and scale drawings by Steve Flint, Ken Gibbons and Mick Nicholson.

Photographs: **Ian S. Carr;** 36T(right): **Colourail;** 10, 42T, 42C, 43, 74T, 86, 91: **Alan Crotty;** 19T: **Ian Fleming;** 11, 63T, 74B: **Steve Flint;** 8, 9, 12, 15, 16, 17T(right), 20-29, 30T(courtesy Railway Modeller), 30B, 31-35, 36T(left), 36B, 38(both courtesy British Railway Modelling), 40, 41, 46, 47T(courtesy Railway Modeller), 47B, 48-50, 51(courtesy Railway Modeller), 52B, 54T, 55-59, 60B, 62, 63C, 65, 66, 67B(left, courtesy Railway Modeller), 68, 69T, 69C, 70T, 70C, 73T, 75(courtesy British Railway Modelling), 78T, 78C, 79, 83B, 84, 85, 89. Also front and rear cover photographs, frontispiece and all preliminary pages: **Graham Gibbons;** 60C: **David Larkin;** 63B, 70B, 72, 81: **Pauline McKenna;** 82B(left): **Dr Michael Rhodes;** 17T(left), 44, 45C(lower), 45B, 52T, 53B(right), 80T, 80C(left), 83T, 96: **Paul Shannon;** 45T, 45C(upper), 54B, 60T, 69B, 80B, 82B(right): **Dave Skipsey & Mike Turner;** 78B(left), 78B(right): **Steve Titheridge;** 67T, 80C(right): **John Vaughan;** 73B, 76(all), 77: **Virgin Railways;** 5.

Below. Reminiscent of 1970s branch line operations in Scotland. Class 24, No 24120, prepares to depart Kyle of Tongue station with the afternoon mixed train for Lairg and Inverness. Kyle of Tongue was built in 1982 to finescale 00 gauge standards and utilised converted and detailed proprietary stock. It was exhibited over an 18 year period before being purchased privately.

Foreword

Perhaps the most striking aspect of the British Rail era was the key role it played in transforming a creaking, high cost nationalised transport network into a profitable and progressive industry. It also represented the longest period in the history of Britain's railways when the aim was to operate them all as a single integrated entity.

To a degree, that aim was realised through initiatives like the old Corporate Image, but BR faced a commercial environment that was constantly changing with increasing ferocity in its later years and the philosophy of one service standard across the whole business portfolio was soon seen as flawed.

Thus, by the 1980s numerous business strategies were adopted in an attempt to meet the needs of the changing markets. Many, such as Sectorisation, were on the whole successful, others less so, but they all gave rise to numerous railway identities, colourful train liveries and new and exciting types of rolling stock in BR's final years.

British Rail had inherited what was essentially an antiquated Victorian network at its inception. Despite all the odds, it did manage to run a modern railway for a modern way of life. It is true that funds were always scarce and investment even more so, nevertheless, rail travel and transport was transformed dramatically over those years.

It is heartening to see that the railway modelling hobby is showing an interest in those times which I was proud to be an active part of. With the help of this book model builders will be able to recreate in miniature many of the faces of British Rail that I witnessed. Aspects such as the Scotrail and Network SouthEast sector identities which brought a fresh new look to the passenger travel side of the business. Other aspects, of course, included the sourcing of new locomotives and rolling stock from overseas manufacturers and whilst the policy was controversial at the time, it created many interesting visual contrasts on our railway scene.

Managing British Rail activities was often an uphill struggle, especially with the media pundits knocking new initiatives or old practices at every twist and turn. Outdated and life-expired hardware and infrastructure made the job ever more challenging too, but the fact that millions of people and tonnes of freight were successfully moved day in and day out is a testimony to all those, in all ranks, who toiled to keep the wheels turning.

Perhaps the railway models that will come to be built in time will reflect a rose-tinted view of British Rail, recalling only the good times and painting an idealistic picture of the scene. If that happens, it should not be seen as a travesty, for making models is, after all a hobby done for relaxation. What is important, is the fact that the British Rail period is being recalled for enjoyment and pleasure and that its place in British railway history is being preserved for posterity.

No doubt in future, I shall be able to say much the same about the modern privatised railway, but that, for the time being, is another story.

Chris Green,
Chief Executive Officer, Virgin Trains.

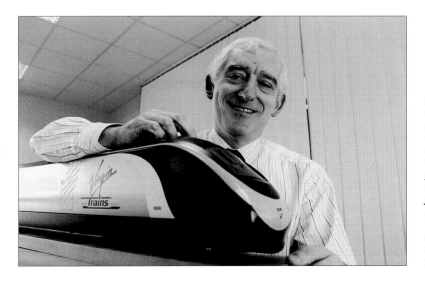

Chris Green has a long and distinguished British railway career. Before his present appointment as Chief Executive of Virgin Trains, he was an influential senior manager within the British Rail hierarchy. His portfolio included General Manager of Scotrail in the early 1980s, followed by General Manager of Network SouthEast.

He is pictured here with a model of the new Pendolino stock soon to be acquired by Virgin Trains for their 21st Century passenger services.

Introduction

Modern Image, what's that?

For as long as the authors can recall, anyone who dared to build a model railway and run diesel or electric locomotives was perceived by the grand old masters of the hobby as someone rather odd and labelled with that now rather bland and misleading title of 'Modern Image Modeller'.

Today that title is widely accepted as synonymous with those who model diesel and electric traction and who build non-steam based model railway layouts. Yet, the steam age railway, which is still a very popular subject for modelling, doesn't have its practitioners labelled with such equally banal and arbitrary titles, as perhaps, 'Ancient Image Modellers'.

Perchance it is that the 'Modern Image' label is seen as a convenient way of categorising anything post 1970. But what is more unsettling perhaps, is that it is often used by the steam age lobby as a way of pigeon-holing all of that modelling they still see as representing the uninteresting or undesirable elements of the railways.

Ironically, with the efforts of most contemporary model railway magazines, the model manufacturers (particularly Bachmann and Farish) and groups like Diesel and Electric Modellers United all doing their bit to promote post-steam era modelling, one could be excused for believing that diesel phobia had finally been stymied. Yet, the old aphorisms describing diesels as 'paraffin cans' and 'blue boxes on wheels' do still echo around the exhibition halls as evidence of an underlying cultural resistance to post steam age modelling.

Although the writers have used the term 'Modern Image' quite frequently themselves, there is now a strong sense that the phrase only serves to reinforce the old and entrenched rivalry of steam vs. diesel. To move this hobby along in the 21st century it's surely time that the image of diesel and electric modelling received a makeover.

Definition of an Era

For over thirty years Britain's railways have been devoid of the steam locomotive. To give that timeframe some sort of perspective, that's a longer period than either the grouping years (1923-1948), or the British Railways steam era (1948-1968). Of course the nostalgia factor associated with the steam railways has much to do with its popularity as a modelling subject and we are not here to debunk or decry such modelling. It is certainly not our intention within this volume to perpetuate the contest between steam and diesel traction. Rather, it is our purpose to throw the spotlight onto a particular period in British Railway history which we believe has been unfairly and unjustly neglected by railway modellers for far too long now.

The period of railway history in question is that 30 year period which began with the Beeching report and ended with privatisation, the period we have dubbed *The British Rail Era*. We believe that the period has been ignored and neglected by modellers not just because of the dislike of modern traction, but because of misinformation, mistaken perceptions, ignorance of the true facts and that ever present simplistic notion that because steam had gone, the railways had somehow, overnight, become boring and uninteresting things.

In many ways it is easy to see why such myths evolved. Certainly, those thirty years witnessed unjust and unfair vilification of real railways from many quarters. The negative aspects of closures and cut backs, rationalisation, investment rationing and technical failure were always headlined and usually ranked alongside the omnipresent music hall jokes about curled-up buffet sandwiches and inaudible station tannoy announcers.

Little wonder then that those years became wrongfully tagged as being years of uninteresting and inevitable decline and ones in which droves of modellers obliviously and unwittingly turned their backs on. Such tragic fogging of the facts has meant that the true potential for modelling this period has never really been fully discovered and realised.

Our aim with this book is to put that to rights, to counter the misconceptions and dispel the legends. We will explore the true facts and extol the qualities and virtues of the British Rail era. Hopefully, we'll demonstrate that the period really is rich in interesting and diverse prototypes and offers tremendous scope and inspiration for all kinds of railway modelling projects.

Optimising Authenticity

The railway modelling hobby has always embraced many diverse interests and levels of model making skill, but one common objective across that broad spectrum has been the desire of the

British Rail freight operations are often characterised by block load trains, as illustrated here with 37101 on a rake of almost identical chemical tanks. The perception is that such operations can be difficult and tedious to model. This book demonstrates various approaches to tackling this subject effectively, especially when space is limited or modelling time is restricted.

Introduction

individual to achieve authenticity and correctness; to create model railways that come as near as possible to looking and being like the real thing and which are operated with complete prototype fidelity. This has been true for the writers too, and is thus a fundemental cornerstone which underpins this book.

Nevertheless, whilst promoting optimum standards and authenticity, we recognise and accept that all individuals model to standards which are within their abilities and resources. For some that may mean ready to run locos and setrack, for others, only the ultimate finescale in S4 or S7 will do. So whilst we shall be advancing the British Rail era as truthfully and authentically as possible, we will not be entering the debate on the rights and wrongs of finescale vs ready to run. Our aim is most certainly to help you get the prototype fidelity right, irrespective of the scale and modelling standards you chose to work to.

Scope of the book

To achieve all of what we have set out in one volume is an almost insurmountable task and to some degree what we have assembled here is only really a part of the story. However, firstly, to provide a sound backdrop, we review the chronological history of the period and examine how the various technical, commercial and political events influenced or initiated all the visible changes which occurred. We have approached this entirely with the modeller in mind so that he or she can readily determine what is correct for a given time or location. It gives a brief summary covering the transformation of locomotive and rolling stock fleets, operating practices and services.

In similar vein, we then look at how the infrastructure of the railways altered covering track, electrification, signalling, buildings, structures and station layouts. Hopefully, we'll lay the ghost of bus shelters once and for all and illustrate that not all goods yards became park and ride schemes.

Passenger and freight services are then considered with especial emphasis on freight. Not just because we like freight stock and freight trains, but because the very essence of modelling the British Rail era is all bound up with the

The High Speed Train was probably British Rail's most noteworthy success and is inextricably linked to modelling main lines during the period. Portraying a long HST set on a layout can be difficult and some plausible solutions to achieving this are presented in this book. The Western Region Main Line was the first to receive production HSTs and a set is pictured here at Cardiff General in May 1978.

metamorphosis of rail freight activity over those years.

With Layout Themes and Schemes we take a look at some of the alternative approaches there are to modelling the period and demonstrate how choice of scale and available space can influence the of choice of format and timescale for a layout.

We have included a few 'shows you how' panels which briefly consider modelling methods, materials and techniques that have a particular and essential role in modelling the railways of the UK in the latter part of the 20th century. These include the choice of products for model buildings, track construction and scenic aspects which are all relevant to the period and help to characterise the image. However, what we must stress and emphasise here is that modelling the British Rail Era is much, much more than just about detailing up and repainting diesel or electric locomotives or stock.

That said, we do recognise that the upgrading and improvement of model locomotives is an important aspect, but we have deliberately not repeated topics which have previously been well covered in other books and magazines. Thus, some recommended works on these subjects (such as adding buffer beam details or etched brass fittings) are listed in the bibliography.

We round off with some appendices and tables of useful information which

will assist the modeller to choose and operate locomotives or units appropriate to the historical or geographical context.

And so into the Twentyfirst Century

Some of the early pioneers of diesel and electric modelling, like Michael Anderton, John Payne, Mike Cole, Terry Onslow and Don Jones all seem to have slipped into relative obscurity, which is a shame, for such people with their various layouts in some way helped to set the agenda for the future.

There are now many who model this period of our recent past and we are pleased to be able to have included some examples of their work to illustrate various approaches and support our crusade. Though, 'crusade' may be too strong a word, we hope that as the hobby moves forward, our collective thoughts in this volume will help many others to discover the true epitome of the British Rail era and finally allow the genre to claim its rightful place in the history and development of model railways.

We commend this book to all those who know and love the British Rail era, and to all those who don't, in the hope that they too will come to share our collective experience.

Chapter One
The British Rail Years

Just what was the 'British Rail' era? To some it was a good example of just how bad a nationalised industry could be, almost a figurehead epitomising a greater national decline, a stooge by which media gurus, politicians and comedians could all score Brownie points off.

To enthusiasts and modellers of the day, the era was all too often likened to the 'dark ages', seemingly for no other reason than the end of steam or the implementation of the nationwide corporate branding.

Yet to many, what it did represent was that period in railway history when, despite the ever steepening odds against it, the system was still doing well the task which it had always done well; that of providing a national transport order for millions of commuters, business passengers, holiday travellers and countless numbers of freight operators.

Historically the 'British Rail' era began at the end of 1964. The popular accepted starting point is with the XP64 project, launched in that year and more than just a hint of things to come. Indeed, almost all express passenger workings, excepting the London - Bournemouth run, were by then in the charge of either diesel or electric traction.

Thirty years on, the end of the era was, officially, the 1st April 1994. On this date the provisions of the Railways Act dissolved the old nationalised system. Beyond that date we will not unduly concern ourselves here, as privatisation itself began a new era for Britain's railways. It is what happened in the meantime that is the subject of this book and this first chapter briefly examines the commercial, political, technological and environmental factors that changed the face of the railways for good and created a whole new and exciting outlook for railway modelling.

Playing with the hand it was dealt.

The British Rail Era did not begin in 1964 with a clean sheet of paper. Rather it emerged out of a confusing myriad of conflicting national and regional aims, objectives, policies and practices. The various railway regions, which had been created following nationalisation in 1948, all still operated much as small independent empires albeit under the collective banner of British Railways. Overlaying all of this were key national strategies that had been developed under plans like the 1955 Modernisation Plan and the 1963 Beeching Report. All these plans and schemes were interlaced with such tangled complexity that the effects were felt at every level of the system and outcomes were often contradictory.

The 1955 plan had acknowledged that 25kV Electrification for all major routes was the ideal goal and should be strived for, despite its high initial costs. This recommendation took a long time to implement and was only ever partly achieved by BR. This though, seems to have been purely because of a lack of finance rather than any lack of will. The long running West Coast Main Line scheme was opened from London Euston to Liverpool and Manchester in 1966, thus coincidentally, and somewhat conveniently giving 'British Rail' a nice shiny shop window in which to display its wares. Glasgow was finally reached in 1974, the wires having slowly progressed northward over the previous four years. But it was to be the 1980s before any other main lines were to be wired up, initially in the Home Counties and East Anglia, and then, what was to prove to be BR's last great project, the full electrification of the East Coast line to Edinburgh.

Other key aspects of the 1955 plan included the replacement of steam traction by modern diesel types and the reshaping of freight movements with the construction of strategically located marshalling yards. Both of these initiatives were largely in place by 1964. Also in 1964, the implementation of 'The Reshaping of British Railways' plan, commonly known as the Beeching Report, was in full swing. The report now represents a legendary watershed in our railway history. The effect of it was more than just the decimation of the system's route mileage and the closure of countless stations, a lot of new rolling stock obtained under the 1955 plan suddenly had to find a new purpose in life. However, the more generally accepted view of the Beeching cuts, that of atrophy and decay, tends to obscure some of the positive aspects of Dr. Beeching's time in office. Chiefly, these were the introduction of Freightliners, and, in

In the early years of British Rail, little outward change was apparent. Steam traction had all but finished but service patterns and the infrastructure were still in a pre-1964 timewarp. Ken Gibbons' New Quay layout epitomises the 1970s scene when the corporate image broom had still to sweep away many of the quaint and modellable ways of old.

conjunction with the National Coal Board and the Central Electricity Generating Board, the introduction in 1965 of the 'Merry go round' system of block train working. Although the sourcing of fuel changed dramatically during the mid 1980s and the Freightliner network survived throughout BR's time (though not entirely in the role as originally envisaged) the continuing relevance of the block train today proves that concept was indeed a sound one.

Soon many diverse industries were shipping or receiving large tonnages by block train and even at one point the waste management industry had its own dedicated landfill trains affectionately known as 'Bin Liners'. However, the common perception amongst modellers is that such block train workings are less interesting and more difficult to model, usually requiring lots of space. Up to a point, that is perhaps true, however the topic is explored in greater depth in chapters 4 and 5.

Back with Beeching, and despite the more upbeat aspects of the report, the more draconian measures it proposed can't, in any way, be ignored.

By the end of 1966, most of the proposed closures had taken place, removing thousands of miles from the network seemingly overnight. Although one or two major lines were involved, the greatest cuts were to the 'traditional' bucolic branch lines, much loved by modellers. These were rendered all but extinct with those that did survive only doing so in a greatly altered and reduced form.

By 1968, the restructuring under the Beeching plan was largely complete and large numbers of displaced locomotives and quantities of rolling stock were effectively redundant. Only a decade or so earlier, under the 1955 plan, there had been a headlong rush into ordering large numbers of different, and often unproven, locomotive types and the apparent folly of that action was now acknowledged by the publication of the National Traction Plan. This was first drafted in 1965, in

light of the redeployment anticipated arising from the completion of the first phase of WCML electrification. It initially concerned itself with efficient allocation of the myriad of non-steam power that BR could now muster. However with the concurrent loss of route mileage and the associated loss of business, it was soon recognised that the plan would need to be revised on a year-by-year basis.

The net effect of the plan was the premature death knell for the less successful diesel electric types, of which there were quite a few, principally the type 1 and type 2 classes for which much of their traffic had gone. By 1968 however, the situation had calmed somewhat, though that year's published plan was to be a memorable one. Long a desire, BR now confirmed that it was to phase out all of the Diesel Hydraulic locomotive types. The decision was based on three factors; the fleet sizes, their engines and their non standard transmissions. Thus the WR's well known Westerns, Warships, Hymeks, and the lesser known Class 22s, were all consigned to early withdrawal. By 1977 all those traction types (bar the class 44s) singled out in the 1968 plan had gone.

From a modellers point of view some of the most interesting and charismatic traction types could no longer be classified as modern image, they had indeed firmly slipped into the realm of

period railway modelling. (for further details see Table 1, page 94)

Returning to 1964, the bulk of the rolling stock ordered under the 1955 plan had been delivered and dieselisation had been completed across large parts of the country. Also by the end of the year steam traction had rapidly become the exception rather than the rule. There were still well known pockets of steam usage though, such as in the North West, Tyneside and on the Bournemouth route.

Despite the decline, general overhauls were still being carried out although the last was that of Britannia Class No. 70013, Oliver Cromwell, which left Crewe Works in February 1967. After then, maintenance was only carried out in the ever shrinking number of steam depots. Coincidental with the redrawing of regional boundaries, and the desire to eke out usable machine life, the old company boundaries, as far as steam locomotives were concerned, became blurred, even forgotten altogether. Thus, in the final years, for example, Black 5s were seen based at Banbury and by now, they, like 8Fs were being treated as 'standards'. The last rites for steam have been dealt with by many books over the last three decades, so all we'll say here is that the last regular workings were on the 2nd August 1968.

The twilight years of steam traction, at those localities where it intermingled with diesel traction, has almost been

An enduring image of the British Rail scene that often discourages modellers is that of the block freight train. Certainly the modelling of such trains often means large layouts and significant expense on identical wagons. Though, as seen in this shot of New Bryford, block freights can be convincingly represented on relatively modest sized layouts.

Steam and British Rail

The perception that steam traction plays no part in the British Rail period is largely over exaggerated.

It is true that steam locos had been banished from many localities and services pre-1964, but it was still around finding work on freight and occasional passenger duties until 1968. Even freight stock usually associated with modern traction was sometimes steam hauled, as this 1966 shot of a 9F hauling 46t oil tankers in West Yorkshire shows.

Preserved steam eventually returned to work so called 'Enthusiast's Specials' on some specified routes and, in time, commercial organisations were running chartered steam trains for corporate promotions and luxury holidays. The modelling of such services has never been popular, but the topic does provide an interesting adjunct for those wanting to include steam in their roster.

overlooked by modellers, indeed, we can only recall it being done once, on Alan Lister's January '68 layout. This is a pity, as it is part of the whole British Rail story and the accurate portrayal of such scenes can be challenging and rewarding.

However, beyond this, steam was still about, albeit in the hands of the preservation movement. Whilst this is itself a separate tale, steam did become relevant again to British Rail upon the lifting of the steam ban in 1971. After then, preserved locomotives hauling steam specials became a not infrequent sight. Perhaps the zenith was to come in the 1980s when BR began to run regular steam hauled excursions over such routes as the North Wales coast, the Settle and Carlisle line and the Fort William to Mallaig branch. Thus modelling the British Rail era does not entirely preclude the inclusion of steam and an excellent example of adopting this approach was seen on Mick Bryan's New Bryford exhibition layout.

Whilst on preservation, comment is

appropriate on the ever growing numbers of diesel locomotives which now fall in this category. However, despite the lifting of the preserved diesel ban in 1993, and the subsequent specials behind class 46, 'Ixion', their relevance to the national network was only to make its mark post 1994.

Understandably, in an organisation of its size, there were often many studies being conducted. The first of the two most notable studies being The Reshaping of British Railways mentioned above. The second was more notable for other reasons. Instigated by Sir Peter Parker, possibly one of BR's most dynamic and memorable chairmen, it was billed as 'the report the railways had asked for'. However, when finally published in 1982, as the Serpell Report, it was greeted with little enthusiasm by anyone, save for the press at the time who concentrated on just one side of the report - this being the part which read like Beeching revisited. In reality the report cited many possible options, ranging from massive increases

in investment to equally massive cutbacks, this latter aspect being that which the media homed in on.

That few, if any, of the report's recommendations were ever actioned was possibly down to them being either unaffordable or unpopular with the public at large. Either way the report had no influence on visible aspects of our railways which are of prime importance to us as modellers.

The Public Image

An essential visible feature of the British Rail era was the implementation across the whole system of the Corporate Image which became immortalised for all time with the standardised blue and grey train livery and the new double arrow logo. There was much more however to the Corporate Image. Certainly it built on the more positive aspects of dieselisation and electrification by capitalising on the brighter and cleaner appearance of the modern stock, but it went much deeper and used design in a co-ordinated way for new developments on all fronts, not just rolling stock.

Totally redesigned uniforms were brought in, a new alphabet for signage introduced, in fact, pretty much everything to do with the public face of the railway was given a makeover. Of course, the new look received its fair share of criticism too, particularly the double arrow symbol which received many a slating throughout 1964/65 for being meaningless and 'non heraldic'. It is ironic, however, that the symbol still survives today as the nationally understood street sign indicating the presence of a railway station!

The Monastral Blue colour scheme was chosen after trials lasting 3 years. Advances in paint technology during the 1950s and early 1960s allowed the successful use of this colour without the trouble of pigment instability. The new colour scheme helped to suppress the old 'company' loyalties which, despite 16 years of nationalisation were still entrenched, and also created a 'look' which was British Rail's own.

Running almost concurrent with the implementation of the corporate image plan was the introduction of the Inter-City concept. Stanley (later Sir Stanley) Raymond set about capitalising on the positive aspects of the recently acquired fleet of type 4 locomotives together with the brand new BR Mk2 coaching stock. The idea was to create a 'product brand' for all main line services. They would be to a single consistent standard right across a designated 'InterCity' network. Track realignments, aimed at improving journey times were an integral part of the philosophy, as well as increased service frequencies.

From 1966 to 1976 improvements in the InterCity business came thick and fast. In 1971 BR was running the first, non supplement, air-conditioned services in the world and the prototype HST was shortly to make its debut. Following the success of this, production HSTs were turned out with BR Mk 3 coaching stock and in 1976 the first services on the Western Region Main Line took to the rails. It was obvious pretty soon after that BR had an excellent new product with the HST and the East Coast Main Line, the NE/SW routes and, eventually, the Midland Main Line were to benefit from their use.

Regrettably however, the HSTs' second cousin removed, the Advanced Passenger Train, was never to prove successful as BR's final 'cutting edge'. Nevertheless, further InterCity development came with the East Coast Main Line electrification, which brought forth the 'InterCity 225' in 1990. With this new concept, use was made of the successful technologies left over from the APT project. Power was provided by the stylish Class 91 and passengers were accommodated in the latest Mk 4 coaches. At the other end of the train, a driving van trailer provided luggage space and the second driving cab. In the new world order of commercialism that the 1990s brought, these new sets had the distinction of being the first BR trains ordered to a 'business' led specification. That is, the railway business managers told the engineers exactly what they wanted, rather than the engineers offering the business managers their latest development!

One small factor that was bound up with the corporate plan and which had a particularly important significance to the modeller was that of locomotive naming. Prior to 1964 many of the first generation diesels received names, notably the type 4 and type 5 classes such as Peaks, Westerns, Warships, and Deltics. Other than 87001, named Stephenson in 1975 in conjunction with the Rail 150 celebrations, no locomotive namings had taken place since 1965, as indeed had been dictated by the Corporate Plan. Then in late 1977, it was announced that the entire fleet of Class 50s and 87s were to receive names. All these names were themed, those for the 50s were based on Royal Navy vessels, whilst the 87s names reflected Anglo-Scottish themes. However the official tags of 'Warship' and 'Royal Scot' class never caught on. After this, it was as though the flood gates had been opened, naming locomotives became seen as marketing and public relations opportunities and pretty much every class of locomotive and HST power car saw some of their fleet honoured in this way. No specific themes were followed however, and whilst, initially, the names applied were dignified, without being stuffy, as the years wore on, 'twinning' with customers' products produced names that appeared at best to be no more than tacky advertisements!

The great strides made with express and main line services were perhaps the most notable of the positive advances made during the BR era. However, we must not forget the more mundane cross country, suburban or local services. Whilst longer journeys tended to be covered by type 2 and type 3 classes hauling coaching stock, many local, suburban and non premium inter-city trains were in the hands of electric or diesel multiple units. One less successful aspect of the corporate image was the initial condemnation of these unit trains to a garb of all over Rail Blue. From a marketing point of view this perhaps reinforced the image that such services were really only a second class means of rail transport. However by the mid 1970s a more liberal view allowed many refurbished types to initially gain a new white and blue livery, though this eventually gave way to the more practical blue/grey scheme by the early 1980s. This relaxation of the earlier strict corporate guidelines was also to benefit locomotives too, but it was at about this time that other factors began to play a part. The Corporate Image that had been about for 15 or so years was about to lose its grip.

Sectorisation or dissection?

Perhaps the greatest management initiative occurred about mid way through the lifetime of British Rail. Some thirty years had passed since nationalisation and only now were the old regional empires and cultures to be

The most noticeable manifestation of Corporate Image policy was with locomotive and train liveries. The heyday of the Monastral Blue look was undoubtably the 1970s. Though often criticsed by modellers for being too standard and boring, it is perhaps a paint scheme that does not demand special skills in its application. Perhaps epitomising the perennial BR image of blue locomotives ond block freight trains is 47 372 with a MGR working on 4th September 1974.

finally swept away. In a major attempt to identify and reduce running costs and streamline the whole business a completely new management structure and hierarchy was developed. This was Sectorisation and it was introduced in 1982, although full implementation took many years.

Under this restructuring, various parts of the railway business were split off into stand alone entities. Concurrent with this new regime, local management were empowered with greater freedom and rather than having to adhere rigidly to centrally decided 'norms' were now able to make their own business decisons.

Under Sectorisation, passenger activities were split into four separate business units each with their own aims, objectives and accountability. These sectors were; InterCity, Scotrail, London and South East (which became known as Network South East from 1986 onwards) and Provincial (which was renamed Regional Railways in 1990). Whilst InterCity and Scotrail quickly launched their new house 'Identities' in 1984, Provincial took until the late '80s to finalise theirs. However, the launch of the Network South East marketing initiative in 1986 really brought home the changing image of BR at this time. The final step into a fully sectorised, business led railway came in 1990 with the announcement that the old regional structure was to be scrapped.

More on the effect of Sectorisation on BR's passenger business and how it affects modelling is dealt with in chapter 3, however, it is interesting to reflect that many in the modelling fraternity at the time criticised the old corporate image for lack of variety and colour. Sectorisation was perhaps their saviour. It unleashed a new epoch of railway liveries which have since been developed under privatisation into a previously unimaginable diversity of colour schemes.

The freight side was also sectorised. Initially set up as a single body under the banner of 'Railfreight', in 1987 it was decided to split this into five core business divisions. These were; Railfreight Distribution (also covering chemicals), Railfreight Coal (trainload and power station), Railfreight Construction (including aggregates), Railfreight

Metals and Railfreight Petroleum. The sub-Sectors were launched along with the triple grey colour scheme and associated livery brandings in a blaze of publicity at Ripple Lane on 15th October that year.

Under Sectorisation, Railfreight was charged with returning this area of business to profit. The rationale encompassed bottom line accountability on the basis that dedicated resources (ie locos, rolling stock and dedicated services) would mean that customers' needs were met more efficiently and cost effectively.

Rational thought

Rationalisation was the one word that was never very far from the pages of magazines commenting on the railways from the '60s to the early '90s. As far as the railways were concerned, it had a very wide meaning, covering literally everything to do with its business. The word suggests the rationing or removal

Rationalistion and new technology sounded the death knell for that most characteristic piece of lineside paraphenalia - the telegraph pole. Although still in evidence in the 1970s, cable trunking and radio signalling finished them off by the 1980s.

of resources and whilst that implied a worsening of service, the reality was that with fewer capital structures to maintain, and the benefits of new technology and new working practices, train services could be retained when they would otherwise have closed.

One early and successful element of this process in the period was the setting up of British Rail Engineering Ltd as a stand alone side of the business to look after the main railway workshops. Sealink, BR's remaining ferry activities, soon went this way also.

Often rationalisation was the result of modernisation, such as the introduction of more PSBs (Power Signal Boxes) and colour light signalling systems. In the mid 1980s the introduction of RETB radio signalling was an example where rationalisation coupled with the introduction of new technology actually helped to prevent far greater cutback effects - such as closure of the routes!

Sadly not all rationalisation had such a benign effect on what would nowadays be called first point of customer contact. In spite of many fine marketing efforts, BR's 'global' image was often not a good one due to these. Many former main lines underwent rationalisation and were singled, this was especially so on the Western Region. This often amounted to no more than lifting the redundant track and sidings leaving disused buildings to collapse and decay, and vast areas, once covered with sidings or locomotive depots, to be overrun by nature. Such tracts became colonised by Birchwood and Rosebay Willow-Herb. Further space for weeds was provided by the large reduction in private sidings, concurrent with the scaling down of many traditional industries. The reduced need, post steam era, to tend embankments also helped the weeds and scrub along. All these factors combined to give a lot of the system a shabby, rundown appearance, definitely not the image as envisaged under the Corporate Plan. In BR's defence however, it must be recorded that there was much to do in order to make the system relevant to the conditions of the late twentieth century and, with financial resources a scarce commodity, tidying up derelict areas was, understandably, very low down on the agenda.

From the modelling perspective those twee little wayside stations with their neat close cropped embankments were now a thing of the past. A layout portraying the BR era would thus have to feature much more luscious undergrowth around the perimeter of the railway fence.

Not all rationalisations meant doom and gloom. Often they were coupled with upgrading, such as that at Peterborough in 1972/3 which transformed the station from a 20mph bottleneck and allowed through services to pass by at speeds of around 100 mph.

After the 1970s the rapid pace of rationalisation slowed. However this isn't to say that it fell out of fashion, it was more that it was now increasingly combined with investment. Compared to

BR's first 15 years, the overall situation on the railways had become more stabilised. Other rationalisation effects due to the introduction of new technology and updated operating practices also occurred. In particular the adoption, in 1971, of the Total Operations Processing System (TOPS) allowed more efficient utilisation of the wagon fleet. As a consequence fewer wagons were required and less siding space was needed to accommodate them when not in service. By the early 1970s improvements with braking systems more often made the use of a brake van redundant. Initially, this led to an agreement with the railway unions to allow the guard to ride in the rear cab of the train engine. Ultimately, of course one man operation was the goal.

The effects of rationalisation on the railway's infrastructure and how it affects the approach to modelling is explored in greater detail in chapter 2.

Acting on instinct

All the above factors which had influenced the way in which Britain's railways had developed after 1964 were essentially internal, that is, the initiatives had been generated from within the industry itself.

External factors, particularly political and commercial ones, began to have an ever increasing influence on our railways as the years progressed.

It is fair to say that in the period under review the effects of several 'Transport Acts' very much shaped and dictated the way in which the modern railway system evolved. There were indeed many such acts, but we'll just concern ourselves here with those which had a key effect on the outward visible image of the railway, such that which are of relevance to the modeller and layout builder.

Though the 1962 Transport Act was passed 2 years prior to the era covered by this book, some of its most important provisions only began to bite from 1965 onwards. One section of this act freed BR from its previous common carrier status and gave management the choice of turning away traffic that could not be carried at a profit. This allowed them to concentrate resources on those activities which could be made to pay, such as block traffics. The National Freight Train Plan of 1966, which championed block trains,

realised that longer, pre-marshalled trains to fewer destinations were far more operationally efficient than the present method of dispatching trains full of wagons for all points north, south, east or west which needed constant remarshalling en route.

A benefit of the new order was the freeing up of line capacity, but it also led to a reduction in the need for so many marshalling yards. This of course varied greatly from the vision within the 1955 Modernisation Plan, though as a lot of money had already been spent, the new sites were retained to act as 'primary yards'.

The 1968 Transport Act came next and also had an effect on railway freight business, leading to a restructuring of the wagonload activities and the formation of the BRS controlled National Freight Corporation. However, it was not to prove to be a final 'cure' for the ails of this traffic as will be examined later.

Possibly more important was the effect of the 1968 Act on passenger services, certainly as far as potential travellers were concerned. The Act clearly recognised that there were some services which were commercially viable, and other services which, whilst loss making, were socially necessary. The Act made provision for grants to be provided by central Government to keep these latter services alive and also led to the creation of Passenger Transport Executives (PTEs) in those areas where Metropolitan Boroughs later came into being in 1974.

Almost without exception, the PTEs subsidised the socially desirable rail services, though in this case, as part of their integrated passenger transport policies. Later, PTEs were to become increasingly involved in rail services, some going as far as 'annexing' them.

The PTEs influence was not just financial however. Each PTE developed its own brand logo and from 1976 onwards these appeared on rolling stock allocated to services within these areas.* However, due to train service diagrams, the branded units often strayed far from their allotted haunts. So even if a layout is not set in a Metropolitan Borough, use

* The 'Merseyrail' branding on MPTE trains appeared in 1971 on Wirral and Southport line electric stock

of such branded units is still justifiable, especially in the north of England and the central region of Scotland. From the mid 1980s some even went as far as having their own liveries. The most notable and widely travelled within its area being the Strathclyde Red (orange) and black.

Returning to freight traffic, as hinted at above, the '68 act did not help the railway solve its freight woes as far as traditional wagonload traffic was concerned. BR management, with their new remit to pick and choose traffics, did feel that there was still money to be made in this area, although some radical rethinking would be needed to make it cost effective. Certainly, however, the writing was on the wall for the 'traditional' goods train.

Help was at hand with the 1974 Transport Act which made provision for Section 8 Grants. This was a huge boost to rail freight activities and changed the associated infrastructure substantially. Essentially if a freight transport activity could meet certain environmental targets by using rail, then a Section 8 grant could be used to subsidise the establishment of new rail links, services or facilities by up to 60% of the total capital cost. Many such opportunities were taken up and new commodity based freight terminals and railheads were constructed. For the modeller, these railheads provide a whole new series of inspiring themes for BR period layouts and the topic is dealt with in much greater detail in chapters 4 & 5. Though not formed as a result of this Act, it is fair to say that BR's Air Braked Network services, and later, the Speedlink Network, introduced in September 1977, capitalised successfully on its provisions.

However, its heyday proved to be short-lived. Speedlink did not qualify for classification under the 1987 sub-Sector restructuring since its traffic patterns were much too diverse. It was combined with Freightliner under the Railfreight Distribution sub-Sector, although the services and 'brand' were retained. Under Rfd, the Speedlink network was used as a catch net for traffic that fell short of an economic block load for the other main sub-Sectors. Sadly the overall decline in wagonload traffic seemed to be unstoppable, and Speedlink was axed in

These logos were applied to stock used on PTE services from around 1976. The overbrandings were perhaps the first chink in BR's Corporate Image and were the precursors of the later 'house' liveries of the 1980s. Transfers in 4mm scale can be obtained, but hand lettering is necessary in other scales.

1991. As modellers however, we need not concern ourselves with the economic practicalities of Speedlink, the principle provides an ideal prototype activity for replication on all sorts of layouts and, as we explore many times elsewhere in this book, offers a wealth of themes and ideas worth modelling.

Freight traction evolution
Throughout the 1970s the block train concept and the MGR system slowly expanded and evolved. The construction boom in the 1970s led to a rapid rise in aggregate traffic and this in turn, combined with the effect of the 1973 oil crisis on the coal and power industries, stretched the available traction fleet to the limit. It even led to the reinstatement of some classes (Warships) and the postponement of the withdrawal of others (class 44). However the need to run heavy aggregate trains, plus the envisaged increase in MGR workings, could not be satisfied in the long term by such stopgap measures. Thus the new requirement for high powered freight traction led to the procurement of the class 56s. The introduction of these freight orientated type 5s - the first of the 'third generation' of diesel power for BR - being in order to keep pace with the increasing workload.

With the usefulness of the type 5s demonstrated, further locomotives of this power rating came in 1983 with the introduction of the class 58s. More

significantly, the politically motivated desire during the 1980s to involve private capital in the railways, led to the introduction of the Foster Yeoman owned GM class 59s. These demonstrated further improvements over the indigenous type 5s and BR freight managers, having observed them from the sidelines, soon cried out for some 'state of the art' heavy haulage locomotives themselves. By now of course, it was no longer a foregone conclusion that British locomotive builders, including BREL, would automatically receive contracts, but despite stiff competition from GM, Brush won the contract for the class 60. The first one, 60001, being delivered on time in September 1989.

Pass the Parcel
From the inception of British Rail, mail and parcels traffic carried on regardless, though it was recognised that train speeds needed to be increased to meet raised customer expectations and also to keep within revised traffic paths. The famous Travelling Post Offices (TPOs), immortalised in the 1930s film 'Night Mail', carried on throughout the BR era, although the last pickup/drop at speed took place in 1971 at Penrith. Slowly, pre-BR parcels stock was disposed of and by late 1986 all parcels trains consisted of purely BR built vehicles. As with all of its traffics, BR tried out various ideas to

improve service and speed up handling. For parcels and mail the 'British Rail Universal Trolley Equipment', known to everyone by its acronym 'BRUTE', proved quite a success, and not just for itinerant railfans to rest their bottoms on!

By the late 1980s BR was at the mercy of many outside influences and huge portions of parcels traffic, including the time honoured national newspaper contracts, had been lost to road haulage and air freight. In 1988 the Parcels Sector consolidated its remaining business and the fight back began. As well as its separate business identity, the Sector had gained its own livery and stock began to appear in Post Office Red with a dark grey band. The relaunched Parcels Sector image was beautifully depicted in the 1988 update of the Night Mail film, yet, hardly before the paint had dried, a second relaunch took place! The Sector was renamed Rail express systems (RES). It continued to consolidate what business it had and despite some developments being stillborn, such as 'Track 29', other initiatives continued to bear fruit beyond 1994.

Parcel traffic has always provided interesting train formations for the modeller and this certainly remained the case during the early British Rail era. The variety was to wane during the mid '80s and parcels trains after that time consisted of solely of BR standard bogie vehicles. However, for the modeller, interest can be found in such things as the short-lived attempt to retain premium parcels and newspaper traffic. Between 1985 and 1988, life expired class 105, 114 and 127 units were stripped out and pressed into service as parcels carriers, the latter two classes even gained roller shutter doors and modified liveries. However the bold experiment was short lived and, not surprisingly, unreliable.

Fortunately for modellers favouring BR in the 1990s, parcels traffic did begin something of a renaissance. By the final years of BR, RES had the bit between its teeth and soon rebuilds and variants of GUVs and BGs appeared. Furthermore, the stock appeared in at least five different liveries, and so, by the time of BR's demise, parcels traffic was once again diverse and interesting.

The Bitter End
Throughout the 1980s the principle of privatisation gripped the nation. Whilst many of the national utility companies were sold off in rapid succession, the Government of the day held off with the privatisation of the railway system. Initially, the already nominally independent Sealink and BREL were sold off but through a lack of serious interest in schemes such as the Settle - Carlisle sell off, together with problems on other fronts, the matter of full privatisation of BR did not seem to be given much serious thought until after the 1992 election. Then it was carried through at a seemingly rapid pace. The Gatwick Express portion of InterCity was set up as a 'shadow franchise' during 1993. This being done to give potential operators an idea of how the 'new order' would be structured, that is with franchisees running the trains whilst the track, stations and infrastructure would be managed and administered by a separate company.

Against this background, privatisation plans forged ahead and the overall strategy became clearer. One surprising aspect was that BR was not to be allowed to tender for any franchises. In 1993 the final BR reorganisation took place, this regrouped all rail freight services by geographical location in line with plans for the impending sell off. Oddly all the earlier changes made under the freight sub-Sector initiatives were effectively swept aside and new freight operator identities were created; Load Haul, Mainline and Transrail.

Some locomotives hurriedly received new liveries in what, in retrospect, looked very much like the arbitrary exercise of papering over the cracks prior to a sale!

Concurrent with privatisation, BR was also having to make provision for the services which were soon to reach these shores via the Channel Tunnel. Plans for an all new rail link to London were drawn up but soon ran into trouble on environmental and social grounds such that when the tunnel opened for business Eurostar trains were forced to creep through the already congested tracks in the Garden of England. Freight workings, on the other hand, very quickly took off and gave railborne freight a much needed boost.

As far as British Rail as a coherent and integrated system was concerned, the official end came on the 1st April 1994. It came with a whimper, rather than the anticipated big bang that some of the privatisation protagonists had expected.

At this date, the system was actually in limbo. Railtrack, the infrastructure operator, was up and running with British Rail still in charge of operating train services. Slowly as more franchises were awarded, it was divested of these duties and now exists in name only.

As for the aftermath of the sell off, that is another matter well beyond the scope of this book.

British Rail is dead......., long live British Rail!

Steve Moore's 56 047 in Transrail livery illustrates how dramatically the embodiment of British Rail had changed in 30 years. The era had begun with the quest for success and quality as an integrated and standardised business, yet it ended its days in a state of multicoloured fragmentation.

Chapter Two
The Infrastructure Revolution

By 1964 Britain's railway 'infrastructure' had only altered significantly on those lines which had been subjected to 15kV and 25kV electrification schemes. Elsewhere, apart from paint schemes and a few more weeds, things were still very much as they had been pre-1948, indeed in many instances, much as they had been since Queen Victoria was Head of State!

A lot of the capital infrastructure; stations, bridges, tunnels and other civil structures, were now well over 100 years old and, often due to expediency, maintenance of many areas had been cut back and rationed over the years. The physical structure of what was still essentially a Victorian railway system would therefore need to undergo radical and dramatic change in order to encompass and accommodate the new economic, social and technological orders that were emerging in the latter part of the 20th century.

Thus the thirty year period from 1964 to 1994, probably saw more numerous and far reaching changes to the railways of the British Isles than the previous hundred years had ever done.

Perhaps the most severe change to any railway line is that of total closure and abandonment, leaving behind just the trackbed and its associated civil engineering structures. In this book we obviously will not be concerning ourselves with what happened afterwards to such lines. However, these closures did have a very real effect on the appearance of the routes left open. For instance, facilities at sites such as junction stations, which no longer operated as junctions, would be left with redundant bay platforms and rusting exchange sidings. Thus for many years afterwards, it was possible to observe along the lineside many weed infested sites of once grand installations, sometimes with track still left in situ. One particularly striking example remains to this day on the eastern approaches to Guide Bridge station. The sidings, disused since the abandonment of the Woodhead route, are still in situ and can be observed amidst the dense undergrowth of flourishing Silver Birch wood.

Modelling such a site may actually seem rather a pointless exercise (pun not intended!), certainly purchasing and laying track that is then simply covered with undergrowth and never used appears to be a waste of effort and money, as would building a baseboard wide enough for modelling the bare trackbed of lifted sidings. Nevertheless, to capture the atmosphere of the time and location in model form, a representation of such neglect ought to be considered.

Completing the circle by the late 1980s, much of the redundant land had finally been sold off by British Rail's property department for use in redevelopment. This was, and indeed, still is controversial, since many perceived that selling off these sites could hamper any future renaissance in railway activity. However, it did have an environmental and aesthetic benefit to the modern railway's appearance, as many long overgrown and untidy sites were transformed into bright new retail parks.

Whilst the preceding two paragraphs may seem to present a negative impression, there is, sadly, no getting away from the fact that except in few cases, the years 1964-94 saw the rail network on the defensive. However, this certainly doesn't mean that what remained was of no interest to the

The Corporate Image vision of BR at Church Fenton in 1991. All track is concrete sleepered and the station fittings include high efficiency lamp standards, glass waiting shelter and new seating. Note, however, the old style of timber fencing.

Diesel Depots

In steam days even the smallest of branch terminii might posses a single road shed with coaling and watering facilities. Under BR, the consolidation of servicing facilities for modern traction became the norm and larger regional based sheds like Toton, Eastfield and Crewe, took the leading roles. Smaller depots, typically of the type most suitable for average sized layouts, did survive in small numbers. Kings Lynn stabling point (left), seen in 1981, contains all the necessary facilities in a compact location, whilst Buxton (below), seen in 1976, occupies a larger area and has been adopted for layout themes many times already.

modeller. In fact, we'd argue that the whole era offers a vast number of different and undiscovered prototype angles waiting to be to explored and reproduced in miniature. Certainly the infrastructure of the British Rail era became unique to the period and some particularly modellable subjects are examined in the following paragraphs and individual topic panels.

Locomotives have long seemed to hold the greatest fascination for many enthusiasts and modellers, so a look at the metamorphosis of the railway's locomotive depots is probably appropriate, and especially since modelling such a prototype is both plausible and achievable for those with limited time, space and money.

Housing the fleet

By 1964 the folly of standing complex machinery next to copious amounts of coal dust, water and ash had long been realised. To get away from this problem, purpose built and suitably modified depots were in the process of being introduced. Whilst much of the rebuilding and re-equipping of depots took place just prior to 1964, it remained

an ongoing process as steam was still in retreat at this date. Re-equipping was to carry on beyond the demise of coal fuelled traction. During the golden twilight of the old order, many of the remaining depots assumed the status of shrines, Rose Grove and Patricroft being notable examples in the North West. Despite steam's latter day fame, the superior productivity and different maintenance needs of diesel and electric traction saw to it that large numbers of depots became redundant. Consequently many were closed, never to see the new traction order in its ascendancy.

Under dieselisation, the rationale of locomotive depot allocation gradually changed and many of those sheds which remained steadily lost their 'allocations' of locos. Their physical appearance was however, often little changed by this, since they were still used for routine maintenance, stabling and fuelling. Often, these sites fell into the category where financial prudence had dictated that total reconstruction was not feasible, and so, appeared little modified from steam days. Birkenhead Mollington Street and Northwich, on the LM region, being two examples of this. The coal and

ash plants disappeared of course, but their places were taken by fuelling points and diesel storage tanks. If nothing else, dieselisation rid them of coal dust and ash, though more often than not, oily grime replaced it.

Sometimes a kind of half way stage was reached, where old structures, suitably modified, were retained to augment new buildings. An example of this would be the DMU depot at Chester, which retained the Chester and Birkenhead Railway's mid-Victorian 3 road shed augmented by a concrete shed (which is supposed to have been the basis of the venerable Hornby Dublo model).

However, in many places, there was no other alternative but to start again. Thus, some old familiar places were changed radically, often the only link being the retention of the name. Willesden depot in north London well illustrates this, the old LNWR site having been redeveloped to cater for both electric and diesel traction. There were even some totally new depots, Finsbury Park, despite its short lifespan is possibly the doyen of these, having achieved fame as the southern home for the Eastern Region's Deltic allocation.

Many of the 'new' depots resulted from the totally different stabling and maintenance needs of unit trains, specifically DMUs, then later HSTs. These have mostly been provided with separate facilities, either adjacent to traction depots, as at Old Oak Common, or on totally separate sites, such as Bounds Green, another North London depot, but this time on the ECML.

Seemingly out of step, as ever, the Western drastically reduced the number of depots and stabling points. They preferred to concentrate on a relatively small number of heavily re-equipped sites which were able to carry out virtually anything bar an engine overhaul. These 'mini-works' were part and parcel of the region's diesel hydraulic 'concept', and, in their use of component exchange repair techniques, foreshadowed the introduction of CEM - component exchange maintenance, (also known as 'cost effective maintenance') to the rest of the system in 1986, long after the last hydraulic had been withdrawn. Portraying the CEM regime on a layout can be achieved using some highly visible cameo scenes. Namely, repaired pieces would have been delivered by road for off loading by fork lift truck leaving the palletised or crated items stored 'in view' for a time on the hard standing. Also, one of the traction depot's dead roads could be commandeered to house a locomotive or unit that was being used as a 'Christmas Tree'; being stripped to surrender its usable items so as to keep others on the go. Creating any of these scenes could provide hours of absorbing detail modelling.

Due to further electrification schemes, changes in operating practices (which included more intensive and elaborate diagramming) and new, low maintenance traction technology, the number of facilities constantly reduced over our 30 year time span. By 1994, the traditional 'locoshed' was all but dead. Even relatively new or recently rebuilt depots were not guaranteed a long life, Finsbury Park and Carlisle Kingmoor possibly being the highest profile casualties of the time.

What remained were large depots, such as Toton, Immingham and Crewe Diesel Depot, these examples catering almost solely for locomotives. There were also large depots whose main work was in catering for multiple units and unit trains, such as Neville Hill (Leeds), and Craigentinny (Edinburgh).

Excepting the larger conurbations of London, Birmingham and Bristol, the WR tended to cater for all traction units on the same site. The three large centres mentioned having sufficient traffic to justify separate locomotive and unit depots. As for the Southern, the electrification schemes of the 1920s onwards had already allowed for some rationalisation. What resulted was a network of car sheds, usually sited at points where services terminated, these not necessarily being terminus stations themselves. As for the regions smallish fleet of diesel, electric and electro-diesel locomotives, these were allocated to four main depots, with fuelling and servicing facilities at just four other locations.

In modelling these installations, it's possible to categorise the facilities as follows. A typical 'traction depot' consisted of a servicing shed, complete with pits, stores, and messing facilities. There would be a fuelling road, together with the associated fuel storage tanks and perhaps some external holding sidings on which to stand locomotives. Larger depots would often have a maintenance shed for heavier work, complete with lifting facilities, together with washing plants and concrete aprons. The rails through the washer being bolted directly to the concrete, since if ballast was used it would soon be washed away.

Some, though very few, retained turntables; mainly, though not always, due to the shed layout being of the 'roundhouse' type, as at St. Blazey.

Not all the buildings were replaced and traditional structures still rubbed shoulders with those of the concrete and steel portal frame type well into the '90s. The latter type of construction became

A HST depot in a small space

With the rise of the unit train, modelling a depot catering for their needs provides a new slant on the shed modelling theme. The facilities for DMUs, EMUs and HSTs tended on the whole to be narrow and long. Coupled with the modern style steel portal frame buildings, they may present an easier prospect to successfully replicate in miniature. In fact, you can buy suitable buildings off the peg in 4mm and 2mm scales. However, you'll need a relatively long space to accommodate HSTs in any scale, but you can use the old trick of modelling only one end of the depot, with a bridge or bypass to hide the other end and exit off stage, as shown here. With short traverser style fiddle yards located at either end, a 4mm layout could be accommodated along a 12ft wall, whilst in N gauge, only 6ft of space is required.

The idea is that only the power car and first carriage of the HST is all that is ever seen just poking out of the end of the shed. Particularly suitable for a late BR period layout, the main lines would see 2 car Sprinters and Pacers and light engine movements for refuelling. Of course, this design is also easily adaptable for use with other types of unit trains such as ECML class 91 electric sets.

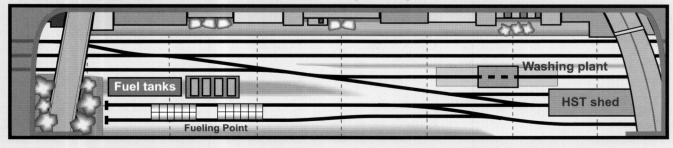

Fuel tanks

Fueling Point

Washing plant

HST shed

the norm during the sixties and evolved into the modular buildings of the 1970s, many of which were used to house the then new HST fleet.

One point to keep in mind is that even a moderately sized depot took up a considerable amount of land, and the kind of facility most modellers might have space for would tend to be one of the relatively rare small depots or a stabling point, like, for example Buxton, which been the inspiration for several layouts down the years. Other such examples would often consist of no more than a convenient, though otherwise redundant, siding plus a hut, or a portakabin for the crew, such as with the Beattock stabling point.

The reduced need for 'engineering' maintenance often led to locos being stabled alongside coaches in carriage sidings. Electrically powered stock being easily dealt with in this way. Here, they could be cleaned and, in the case of passenger stock, replenished with water. Furthermore, the ease of dealing with modern stock, plus the greater availability demanded from it, often led to the lay-overs and internal cleaning being carried out in station platforms. Thus, the need for traditional carriage

sidings and sheds diminished, the numbers of these shrinking drastically during BR's time.

Contrary to the impression the foregoing may give, some investment was made and automatic cleaning plants became universal at the carriage sidings that remained. A feature often missed by modellers are concrete 'cleaners' platforms, water standpipes and hoses which were to be found at any depot or sidings where coaches needed servicing. These abounded at even the smaller, more modellable sites. Paul Wade's Maidstone Barracks layout (right) featured EMU servicing facilities and included many of the items mentioned above.

Signalling the way ahead

With the move towards higher train speeds during the sixties and seventies, much resignalling work to the system was carried out. This often entailed re-siting signals to allow for the greater stopping distances required. Although this didn't require the use of colour light signals as an absolute necessity, it was considered desirable. Also by this time, the technology had been developed for controlling a very large area from a single remote signal box, or Power Signal Box

(PSBs), as they were tagged. Colour light signals had themselves evolved into MAS, 'multiple aspect signals', to give them their full title, incorporating two, three or four lamps in one housing. These alone were capable of signalling the railway in a more flexible way, and so, where a large stretch of line or a complete area was to be re-equipped, it made economic sense to fit MAS controlled by PSBs. However, despite the desirability of the use of PSBs, they were never to become completely universal. The reason

Fratton EMU Washing Plant

Automated carriage washing plants became numerous in the 1960s and were built adjacent to carriage and MU servicing areas. The simplest type with rolling vertical brushes bears a resemblance to a car wash! Fratton washing plant near Portsmouth is a more involved affair but could used on a layout with extensive stock servicing facilities. Equally, with selected use of bridges, etc., as scenic breaks, the plant could be a central feature on a minimum space layout suited to those who are interested in just building or collecting EMU/DMU stock.

All change at the station

Under the British Rail regime, the 'Station' became regarded as the initial point of public contact and, as an aspect of the Corporate Image plan, BR aimed to rid itself of the old fashioned, draughty images associated with such places.

Concurrent with the WCML electrification scheme many of the stations on that route were extensively rebuilt, from the small sites, such as Runcorn and Hartford, to what was intended to be BR's jewel in the crown, Euston. Though undoubtedly 'modern' in the sixties' idiom, the fact is, that the architectural style dated quickly and the sites soon became seen as being less than 'customer friendly' despite the very real improvements that had occurred for both passengers and staff alike.

However the 'brave new world' exemplified by the West Coast Main Line rebuild was not typical of this time. Often as a result of rationalisation a lot of once magnificent stations were left as if in the twilight zone. Examples which spring to mind include such places as Bradford Forster Square, Halifax, Liverpool Exchange and, perhaps the grandest of them all, the

It was years before the Corporate Image branding was fully implemented in some localities. Bury, seen here in 1978 (right), still exhibits the old 1950s British Railways signage, albeit rather tatty and vandalised. Other extremities of the network were also so treated. On the Kyle line blue totem signs could still be seen in 1981, and even though they had gone by 1986, other platform furniture, such as the pre-nationalisation luggage barrow at Garve (below), was still around.

original Snow Hill station in Birmingham. This latter place during its last 5 years, until March 1972, existed solely for an infrequent single car DMU service to Wolverhampton.

With their smoke begrimed fabric and fading '50s British Railways signs, these stations stood in stark contrast to the image that BR wanted the public to see. However despite, or maybe because of, the decay and dereliction, they often retained

for this being that in areas of relatively light traffic, the high initial capital investment of such schemes where far greater than any potential cost savings. That said, whilst in 1964, the majority of railway signalling was still mechanical semaphore, 22 years later, all of BR's main lines had been converted to MAS, mostly under the control of PSBs. The exception to this rule being the southern section of the WCML electrification system, which, whilst using MAS, is still controlled (though not for much longer) from re-equipped, conventional LNWR/LMS signal boxes.

Even in areas where semaphores were still dominant, the ability to site colour lights remotely was taken advantage of and many conventional boxes were thus used to control signals a long distance away from them. In consequence, in a sort of mini-PSB scenario, one central box was retained, taking over the duties of several adjacent ones which were demolished.

Even as recently as 1994, semaphore signals and traditional signalboxes were still numerous enough countrywide to be classed as commonplace. In fact, during the '60s and '70s, many semaphores had been renewed like for like. One twist to this was where old regional boundaries had been redefined. Here, the new controlling region's standard issue was

often used to replace (though not always in a wholesale manner) those of the area's former masters. Hence, WR pattern lower quadrant signals appeared on former Southern lines, Midland upper quadrants on Western lines, etc. This mixing of differing companies/regions fittings presents an interesting prospect for the modeller, much in the way that the old regional boundaries for locomotives and rolling stock became blurred from the 1980s onwards.

By the end of our chosen time span, the largest remaining concentrations of semaphores were around Worcester, Humberside, parts of the North West and Lincolnshire.

All change at the station (cont.)

a forlorn and lamentable dignity. Yet often the unused track beds and platforms became makeshift overspill car parks - certainly ironic, as BR was unwittingly catering for those individuals who had long abandoned rail travel!

To a modeller interested in the years 1965-75, recreating such a station in miniature could form a very absorbing project. Whilst the railway element would probably be a little prosaic, capturing the atrophy and desolation would be an intriguing artistic challenge.

The mid '70s onwards were to see a change in the fortunes of many of these faded gems and gradually, often with local authority assistance, the buildings were cleaned up and renovated. Any redundant areas were then either fenced and sold off, or tarmaced over to provide improved car parking, the railway by this time realising the value of good facilities in enticing the motorist to travel by rail.

By contrast, out in the sticks, many small town and wayside stations became unstaffed. At the very least, this left the buildings subjected to the perils of weather and vandalism. However, the railway still had the duty to maintain them in a safe condition, whether used or not, and in the longer term,

cost dictated that very many buildings were either sold off or simply demolished. Even once large stations, such as Church Fenton on page 16, succumbed to 'Bus Shelters'. Such rationalisations often led to localised, short term outrage, but in the face of increasing costs, these economies, however aesthetically unpalatable, made the difference between the survival of a basic service or complete closure.

We, as modellers of this period shouldn't be too critical though, since for those of us short of modelling time, a bus-sheltered station can provide a quick solution for accommodating our miniature communities! That apart the fact that many 19th century rural station houses are now in private ownership means that they are still very much part of the railway scene and still need to be incorporated on the model.

At those localities where station buildings had to be replaced on a like-for-like basis, BR, unlike the old companies, did not have a common 'style' of architecture. Indeed, the five regions seemed to be left alone almost to 'do their own thing'. Functional concrete and glass formed a common thread to the architecture of those stations rebuilt throughout the '60s and '70s, though in fairness to the architects, they would have only been following

Many older stations, particularly larger urban and provincial ones like Portsmouth (left), had their original fabric refurbished and survived to be fitted out with all the mod-cons of the modern railscene. Others, like Thirsk (below) seen in 1992, were fully rebuilt in new style from the platform up.

Although large numbers of conventional signal boxes had been removed, some new manual boxes were actually constructed between 1964 to 1994. These were to the controlling region's standard design, though, it has to be said that the aesthetic standards of those examples from the '80s onwards left something to be desired; they were no more than twin storey modular portable cabins. However, their ultra functional architecture does rather play straight into the potential modeller's hands.

Another feature for the modeller to be aware of are the many ground frames installed during this era. Increasing numbers of these replaced signal boxes

where access to relatively lightly used sidings was needed.

Long an essential part of signalling, telegraph wires began to be buried in concrete lineside troughs across the whole system from the late '60s onwards. Whilst there was no specific pattern to the removal of telegraph poles, those lines where upgrading, or resignalling was carried out, tended to be dealt with first. Further changes to cable routing came in the mid '80s, when the rules for passing them under trackwork were relaxed. Previously, these had been routed in concrete troughing, however, from this time, the cheaper alternative of using plastic trunking was allowed. As a

concession to safety the tubing used was Dayglo Orange in colour.

Portable cabins, ever practical, found further use as relay rooms, often next to conventional boxes that controlled colour lights. Their temporary nature allowed easy removal and re-use, whilst at other more permanent sites windowless brick kiosks were constructed as illustrated by the example at Markinch (overleaf).

Whether a line was conventionally signalled or not, AWS (automatic warning system), which had been recommended as result of the 1952 Harrow disaster, finally became all but universal during British Rail's tenure. ATC, the Western's own design being

All change at the station (cont.)

A surprisingly large number of former station houses on surviving rural branch lines were sold off for use as private residences. Eggesford (left) is one particularly well executed example and the station still exudes much modelling charm. Bus-shelter style passenger accommodation is neatly provided on both platforms. Sadly, the station house at Reedham Junction (below left) has fared significantly less well.

were not brought into line with the new signage until the early 1980s.

As well as providing more on-platform information boards, TV monitors were used to augment and display relevant passenger information from the 1980s onwards. As for the minutiae of stations in this era, seats, clocks, barrows, lighting, etc., there was still great diversity well into the early '80s and even later on secondary lines. Often these items were carry-overs from the days of the 'Big Four' and as such, the modeller can use carefully selected items of these 'durables', to give a layout a definite sense of time and place even before placing the stock on it. With such a diversity, it's probably best to study photographs and books relevant to your appropriate time and region to ascertain just what the mix was.

We surely cannot leave this topic without mention of the omnipresent BRUTE trolley. Introduced in the mid '60s, its contribution to the image of British Rail on provincial stations, until its final demise in the late '80s, is now legendary. Fortunately, at least in 4mm, these are available in the form of a simple etched brass kit, being designed to be glued together.

Being so ubiquitous, they're probably best modelled at least in pairs. Their normal haunts being the areas of stations where parcels were dealt with though some did stray to platform ends for use as ad-hoc seating by rail fans of the era. A couple of long haired, flare bedecked youths making use of a BRUTE in this way would make a truthful and amusing cameo, redolent of the 1970s, and a change from the more usual parcels and packing cases.

contemporary ideas. This echoing of architectural fashion was to return to the railways from the mid '80s onwards with the use of more conventional shapes and materials. Good examples of these being the new buildings provided at Tiverton Parkway and Thirsk (overleaf).

Other improvements were implemented under the British Rail Corporate Plan. Most notable were the adoption of the new Rail Alphabet -

corporate black-on-white signage - and new staff uniforms, all of which began appearing from 1965. Old fashioned ticket and information offices were to be transformed into bright and airy 'travel centres'.

However universal adoption of these initiatives took many years to accomplish, pre-1964 uniforms still being seen into the mid '70s, and many stations, particularly those on the extremities of the network,

phased out during the 1970s. When modelling a line that is meant to be fitted with AWS, the actuating magnets will need to be installed between the running rails ahead of the signals. The spacing

was always dependent on the line speed and braking distance of the fastest trains using the line. Consequently, AWS magnets on high speed lines are placed further ahead of the signals than those

on a line where speed is restricted. In reality, the distances involved can be very long and, due to the space restrictions faced by modellers, it's often not feasible to install these in their correct locations.

Above. AWS magnets and protective ramps are actually fairly complex affairs, as this illustration shows. Often the units will be found in an oil begrimed condition.
Right. A feature of the lineside in the BR era is the brick relay kiosk, such as this one at Markinch.

However, on loops and platforms they may be also present. Careful study of contemporary photos of your chosen area will provide guidance here.

The final development in signalling was the introduction of radio signalling, or RETB as it is known. This uses on board radio sets in conjunction with computer based interlocking to control train movements.

It was first introduced in the mid 1980s and its low cost and high reliability make it ideally suited to long remote branch lines, such as the Far North line to Wick and Thurso and the Central Wales line. The obvious effect on modelling is that the lineside is completely devoid of signals, signal boxes and telegraph poles,

Lastly, but by no means least, level crossings were also to see many changes. By the early 1990s, the largest

Below. A detail shot of one side of an Automatic Half Barrier type of level crossing.

concentration of conventional gated crossings was to be found in Northern Lincolnshire, the old order being still visible at Medge Hall, Elsham and Ulceby, to name but three. This area being ironically the one in which the very first automatic half barrier had been successfully tested, near the village of Stallingborough.

Further irony comes with the fact that the Eastern and former North Eastern regions were BR's pioneers in the modernisation of level crossings. It was the NE region who were the first to introduce lifting barriers during the mid 1950s, though these were manually operated from a signalbox. Another type peculiar to lines on this region are the 'Boom' type gates. In operation, the gate is basically an updated version of the traditional style crossing gate, but which rotate on solid-rubber wheels powered by an on-board electric motor. In appearance however, they resemble a low picket type garden fence painted red and white! A feature of their construction was the extensive use of timber and ply, the main boom itself being a plywood box girder. In terms of design, these seemed to be a dead end, and, in the event, lifting motor operated barriers were to prove to be more successful.

By the mid 1960s, all regions had need to upgrade level crossings and from this time, when the crossings came up for modernisation, the type of new installation depended on the degree of road traffic to be catered for. In general, Motor Controlled Full Barriers, (MCBs) are used at busy locations and can often

be operated remotely with the aid of CCTV to the relevant box.

Next down the scale are Automatic Half Barriers, most of these being actuated by the approaching train travelling over a treadle. Open crossings have no barriers fitted and tend to be used in areas where traffic is sparse. These are generally provided with flashing warning lights for road users, whilst those without any lights are subject to stringent train speed restrictions.

Features common to all types of crossing, whether fitted with lifting barriers, boom gates or, indeed, open crossings, is the installation of cattle grids around the track either side of the road and the peripheral white painted palisade fences. Such features that need to be faithfully reproduced if authenticity is to be achieved.

Not all crossings were refurbished with modern equipment. When the Bridlington to Hunmanby route in East Yorkshire was singled, the crossing at Bempton station was reconstructed with traditional gates and a small interlocking lever frame, as the illustration in the panel overleaf shows. This crossing is still in use in this format to this day.

Before leaving the subject of level crossings, the large increases in road traffic of the '60s and '70s often led to great congestion at heavily used ones, particularly in urban areas, and many such were replaced by road 'flyovers'. In some cases leaving the original signal cabin still in situ beneath the new road! Thus providing a new angle on scenic breaks perhaps?

The changing permanent way

Whether you are modelling high speed main lines, Scottish urban networks or meandering freight branches, this is the one topic that just cannot be overlooked.

Whilst proprietary 00 gauge flexible track and pointwork, such as Peco Streamline, makes for quick and convenient tracklaying, those who wish to achieve a higher degree of fidelity in their permanent way must delve further into the subject.

Chaired track with bullhead rail and timber sleepering had been used virtually exclusively on Britain's main railway network since the early days. It was in the 1940s that spiked track using flat bottom rail began to appear due, in the main part, to advancements with both securing spikes and sleepers.

Early flat bottom track in the UK still used wooden sleepering, but with a baseplate and spikes, instead of a chair, to hold the rail in place. By the mid 1950s flat bottomed rail had already become the standard for any new relaying schemes and by the early sixties, concrete sleepers and new flexible track clips were being used almost exclusively when main lines were re-laid.

A further refinement was developed at around this time by the welding together of the rail sections to produce Continuous Welded Rail, CWR for short. With this system, the need to tighten fishplate bolts regularly was dispensed with and, in theory, it provides a far smoother ride. However, allowance has still to be made to cater for expansion and suitable joints are provided every half mile or so. Over our review period, CWR and concrete sleepering gradually displaced bullhead track. It certainly didn't mean however the overnight banishment of bullhead rail and some has even survived on secondary routes and branch lines into the 21st century!

A glance at most sidings will confirm that the use this type of rail is still very much alive.

Despite the increased use of concrete sleepers for running lines, pointwork continued to be constructed from timber sleepering. The reason for this being the extra resilience which timber possesses, vital with pointwork, since it does take a bit more punishment than plain track. However, it hasn't all been a case of 'as you were' in this field, areas of progress include the introduction of cast Manganese Steel crossing noses (see panel) producing a very strong single unit. Also as junctions were remodelled, some very large radius pointwork was introduced, an early example being Weaver Junction.

During the 1970s their use became widespread, the Western Region using them extensively when remodelling the London-Bristol line just prior to the introduction of HSTs. High speed ladder junctions using such pointwork allow

Road Crossings on the level

Level crossings witnessed significant changes in the BR era but present the modeller with simplified alternatives to traditional swinging gate systems.

The AHB crossing as illustrated on Ascott-under-Wytchwood (left) became used widely on high speed lines where road traffic is relatively light. The equipment can easily be modelled in static mode from plasticard offcuts and tube, although working versions can be adapted from continental products.

On branches and secondary routes, traditional crossing gates were still quite widespread, although operated by a lever frame, rather than a box, as the example at Bempton in 1984 shows (below left).

Where road traffic is light and line speeds low, open crossings without barriers were the preferred option, as at Auchterneed in 1990 (below right).

White painted palisade fencing and cattle grids became common features on all crossings.

Pointwork

Even on high speed routes with concrete sleepered track, pointwork still mainly utilises timber ties. However, fabrication methods differ from the days of Bullhead track. Over the review period integrally cast Manganese-Steel crossing noses and wing rails (frogs) became more common (right). Also the practice of bolting check rails and closure rails to adjacent stock rails (below) took over from traditional methods. The modeller using flexi-track, may find such details rather esoteric, but fine-scale enthusiasts seeking optimum authenticity would need to take heed of this, particularly in the larger scales.

trains to switch from the main lines to the relief lines and vice versa at speeds of up to 70mph, the benefits to journey times alone fully justifying the expense. Also around this time, the ECML was undergoing a slow upgrade, though this was as much to make full use of the potential of the Class 55s, as to make ready for HSTs. In common with all line upgrades of the time, heavier ballasting and super elevation became the norm. On the ECML, bedevilled with curves, speed limits were raised by re-alignment, often using the sites of redundant sidings, or sometimes by rebuilding, such as at Peterborough. A further aspect of upgrading was the increase in loading gauge clearances on lines carrying container traffic. Due to the relatively high cost of bridge replacement, the preferred method, where structures allowed, was to lower the trackbed.

However, not all lines justified such expenditure, and often, money was spent in actually reducing the amount of track and simplifying junction formations in line with the traffic patterns of the time. Single lead junctions became common, even where a double track main line diverged. The rationale was that the reduction in pointwork was ultimately cheaper to maintain, though the effects of these pieces of track seeing double the amount of traffic over them, do not appear to have been recognised at the time. Still, this is another case where real life plays into the modeller's hands, as these simplified junctions (as shown on page 25) are far easier and cheaper to build and wire up than a traditional double junction with diamond crossing! These simplified track layouts had a beneficial effect at stations too, allowing bi-directional running through the platform roads and aiding operational flexibility. Obviously such lines would be suitably signalled to allow these types of manoeuvres.

From the mid '60s, many former main lines had assumed a less prominent and less profitable place within the network and many were singled. The rationale was again cost saving, in order to keep the line open at all. Though by no means its own preserve, the Western Region seems to have been in the forefront of such singling. Specifically, the Exeter to Salisbury, Oxford to Worcester, and Princes Risborough to Aynho lines were so reduced. Though much criticised at the time, these lines remained open, and towards the end of British Rail began to enjoy better fortunes.

As much a part of the permanent way as the track were the many thousands of ancillary lineside fittings and notices such a mileposts, speed boards, bridge plates, trespass signs, etc. BR operated a common sense, frugal approach with such fittings, and excepting speed restriction signs, they were only replaced when necessary or life expired. If you look carefully, many pre-British Railways

Simplified Junctions.

Simplified track layouts at junctions became used widely in the review period

Double track to single track junction.

a) Traditional

b) Modernised

Double track to double track junction.

a) Traditional

b) Modernised

In each case, the modernised version eliminates the use of diamond crossings

Bright Sparks - Overhead Line Equipment

The dawn of the 'blue' era was to see the completion of Britain's biggest 25kV electrification scheme to date on the southern part of the West Coast Main Line. Started in 1959, the first phase from London to Liverpool and Manchester was complete with all routes, including the lines through Birmingham and Wolverhampton, energised by 1967.

The Overhead Line Equipment (OHLE), or catenary, used on this early section was very heavily engineered. This is evident from the lineside with lattice girders being predominant in the construction of the supporting masts. Similar structures had been used for the Essex and Glasgow suburban schemes dating from the early 1960s.

The later phase of the WCML scheme, from Weaver Junction northwards, used a lighter design of support, such as shown right. At multiple track sites, RSJ girders are used for the masts with transverse suspension cables supporting the conductor wires. This style became much the norm for future schemes such as those on the East Anglian and ECML routes.

For the modeller, overhead line equipment does present a very interesting challenge and whilst the lighter structures can be represented by judicious use of proprietary models from continental firms, such as, for example, those produced by Sommerfeldt (in 2mm & 4mm), a great deal of scratchbuilding would be needed to portray the installations dating from the 1960s. Examples of both structures have been modelled by the Nottingham (Bulwell) Model Railway Society whose layouts, 'Deepcar' and 'Carstairs Jnct.'

represented the 1500V dc system and the 25kV ac system respectively.

Overall, the subject is a complex one and a detailed study is beyond the scope of this book, however, with the various advances in prototype design made over the years, careful study of the relevant OHLE from photographs would be beneficial in aiding their replication.

The illustrations taken from the lineside show examples of both the heavier and lighter constructions.

Above left. Catenary on the first phase of the WCML was heavily engineered and incorporated a lot of lattice girder supporting gantries.
Above right. In contrast, most electrification schemes from 1968 onwards, used lighter supporting structures as shown here on the ECML.

and even pre-Grouping items still exist to this day. Speed signs however did get replaced on many mainlines. The old style yellow painted cut-outs gradually being superseded by road style boards.

Commonly these replacements were triggered by the introduction of differential speed limits on a line, the latter being part of the total package of Sprinterisation.

Before leaving the topic of the permanent way, one further aspect needs to be considered - that of weeds. Briefly mentioned in the second paragraph, this was, if you'll excuse the pun, a growth

Bright Sparks - Third Rail

We must not of course neglect third rail electrification schemes, especially as third rail SR modelling has witnessed a marked increase in popularity in recent times.

To the north of London however, things were rather different for 3rd rail systems. The ex-NER Tyneside suburban lines were de-electrified in 1967, probably as much to do with the then emerging surplus of DMUs as the need to renew the supply equipment. In the late '70s many of these routes became integrated into the Tyne and Wear Metro system which uses overhead current pick up.

Another 3rd rail line subject to metamorphosis was the Manchester to Bury line (pictured on page 20). Originally electrified by the L&Y in 1915, it survived through much of the British Rail era as rather an interesting enigma until it became a fundamental part of the Manchester Metrolink project in 1991.

Two 3rd rail networks that fared rather better, in terms of retaining 'heavy' rail status, are those that nowadays form Merseyrail. Indeed, these have been expanded, with the Wirral lines now running to Chester and Ellesmere Port, and the old Southport to Liverpool line having been linked up to the ex-CLC line with electric trains now running as far as Hunts Cross.

In 4mm, many 3rd rail unit types are available as kits from DC Kits, whilst Peco produce parts for replicating the conductor rails.

area. Abandoned sidings soon began to return to nature. Concurrent with this, embankments and cuttings began to sprout much of the same, all as direct result of the reduced maintenance regime brought in after the end of steam.

Chief among the weeds to colonise the embankments was Rosebay Willow-Herb and a tract of this along your layout's frontage is as good an indication of the modelling period as is the colour of your rolling stock! Synchronous with the weeds, many trees and shrubs also began to sprout and establish themselves. As the years passed, these became more of a nuisance adding the menace of leaf fall from trees beyond the railway boundary. Leaves on the line, of course, have become deeply enshrined in British Rail folklore, and to combat the problem, an adhesive mix called Sandite, a mixture of wallpaper paste and sand, was spread onto the track by specially modified stock.

Beyond the fringe

Although we've already touched on the subject of disused railway land in the preceding text, the subject of selling off land only really became noticeable from the 1980s onwards.

The BR property board had much earlier earmarked those redundant sites which once housed loco depots or marshalling yards. Whilst a great deal had already been sold off, the economic boom time of the 1980s accelerated the rate at which disused railway land was redeveloped.

It provided space for the many shopping parks and factory estates that began to spring up, plus of course, income for the railway. In large conurbations, where the railway had reduced in width, corridors of land were sold off to provide space for new roads which were deemed necessary to combat ever increasing traffic congestion. Whilst roads and the attendant traffic are always difficult to model convincingly, a low relief backdrop of small factory units, built up from Wills or Pikestuff cladding sheets, would help to create the setting for a late British Rail period layout.

It's also perhaps a good point to mention that despite selling a good deal of ex-railway land, BR still had legal ownership of the sites of many closed railway lines. With this came their

Leaves on the line! The neat close-cropped embankments associated with Britain's steam age railways are no more. Trees and shrubbery now grow right up to the edge of the trackbed especially on lightly used lines such as illustrated here on the Flixborough branch.

obligation to maintain bridges and viaducts that had stood idle, at least as far as railway use is concerned, for many years. Not surprisingly, many of these were demolished, though this policy couldn't be adopted wholesale, since many had been classed as listed structures. Since then, many have been disposed of to local trusts, or councils, especially where their historic or aesthetic value is deemed to be important. For the British Rail modeller, these bridges can provide a way of hiding running lines as they run 'off stage'. They could be depicted as being trackless and derelict, or as cycleways or walkways.

And finally.......

You'll have no doubt by now grasped the enormity of this subject, and how, slowly but surely regional railway differences were eroded, even before the final abandonment of the regional structure in the early 1990s.

You may well have your own particular perspective in terms of what the railway infrastructure means to you. So, to use an old, over-hackneyed maxim, 'careful study of photos will help'. Only next time, take a peek well beyond the rolling stock!

Chapter Three
Passenger Train Portfolio

The rise and rise of the unit train

The story of the passenger train in the British Rail era is underpinned by one consistent trend, the steady rise of 'unit train' formations. This manifested itself with increased provision of diesel and electric multiple-unit stock, followed by the fixed formation High Speed Train sets and latterly with increased push-pull working of conventionally hauled stock, also in fixed formations.

The trend offers many advantages to the full size railway, such as the cutting down of shunting movements at terminals, whilst on the other hand, it has an inescapable effect on the modeller.

Foremost in this story are the large fleet of first-generation (latterly called 'Heritage') DMUs introduced under the Modernisation Plan. Although originally intended to be cheaper and more efficient trains for branch and local services, this aim was not fully achieved because of associated costs with depot provision. Consequently, changeover to DMU operation usually extended to secondary and local workings in a given area, rather than on branch lines in isolation.

The DMU concept was also developed for fast, light transport between major cities and also on some lengthy cross country routes. The end result was that certain areas on the British Railways network developed concentrations of DMU workings, a state of affairs which more or less persisted unchanged throughout the first twenty years of British Rail.

Equally influential in the evolution of the unit train were the various electrified networks which British Railways inherited in 1948. The former Southern Railway, in particular, had an extensive system of third-rail electrification in place in the South East on both main and branch lines. This was extended piecemeal throughout the British Railways period and virtually all domestic passenger trains on this system became worked by EMUs.

On the Western Region, the classic 'Blue Pullmans' were conceived as 'unit trains', rather than 'multiple units' in the accepted sense. They are also generally accepted by many as being forerunners of the HSTs. The HSTs will be familiar to everyone as the one-time flagships of the InterCity fleet. Since their initial introduction on the Western Region and East Coast main lines, they steadily spread onto various other routes and, more than anything else, heralded the end of the conventional locomotive-hauled main line train.

The push-pull concept had been very much limited to local and branch line working in steam-age Britain. However, since the 4-TC/4-REP sets of the 1967 Bournemouth electrification, the mode has enjoyed varied development on several high-speed routes and now operates many long distance services on both West and East Coast main lines.

Although the succession of the unit train over the last 30 years does appear to have been unremitting and universal, a renaissance of conventional locomotive hauled passenger trains did occur right in the middle of our review period and is covered in greater detail on page 37.

Little and often

It would be a fair generalisation to say that passenger train formations on all routes have shortened over the years whilst frequency has increased. The basis being that more frequent travel opportunities satisfy market demand more effectively. Consequently, operating practices have tended towards the running of fleets of standard formation trains and away from the old ways of providing bespoke train lengths that suited particular loadings at certain times of day. This has been especially relevant in the latter years of our review period when 'Sprinter' sets became prevalent on many routes.

The principle has obvious benefits for the modeller, in that smaller main line layouts involving more intensive operation can now appear authentic.

Another factor affecting train length has been the move away from on-train full meals service. Longer distance expresses in the classic diesel and electric period included at least one vehicle given over to catering, but by the late 1970s, micro buffet conversions from ordinary stock were replacing traditional buffet cars. The widespread move to franchised trolley operation in the Sprinter era needs no modelling input, unless you want to portray the trolley and its attendant on the platform changing trains!

In the following sections we consider how the preceding trends and progressions affected passenger services on different parts of the system and reflect on the prospects for representing them in model form. We have loosely grouped the services into convenient categories, namely; main line, provincial, commuter and branch line operations. There are many exceptions and overlaps between the broad divisions of category, but overall, the basis is sound and reflects the way many British Rail modellers already approach the subject.

The succession of the all conquering 'unit' train concept is exemplified by the second generation DMUs which spread to all parts of the network after their introduction in the late 1980s. Their modern designs do make interesting contrasts with aspects of the old order, such as in this shot of a class 158 passing semaphore signals and a pre-Grouping NER lineside notice in East Yorkshire.

Main Line Modelling Interpretations

Modelling a modern electrified main line in the British Rail era will be almost exclusively associated with the West Coast route which became fully operational to Glasgow by 1974. In contrast, the whole East Coast route was not fully wired until the final years of BR. Here 86260 runs into Penrith station in September 1977. The 0000 headcode being indicative of the mid 1970s.

South Wales in 1976, being extended later to the West Country.

The strong positive images created by the HST became ever more important to the BR marketing men and by 1980 even the North-East/South-West and Midland main line services were considered significant enough to warrant HST stock despite few sections of the routes being suitable for 125 mph running.

Locomotive haulage lingers on

Whilst the major ready-to-run manufacturers offer HST sets in a multitude of guises in both 4mm and 2mm scales, there are many modellers for whom the units offer little stimulation.

Fortunately there are other main line scenarios well beyond the territories of the HST that can provide inspirational subjects for layouts. Some routes, even to the Capital, have played second fiddle for locomotive and rolling stock allocation and their generally shorter train formations present a possible compromise for modelling.

On the Great Eastern section, the Liverpool Street to Norwich and Cambridge lines had been an early pioneer of regular interval services with nine coach sets, even in the Britannia era of the 1950s. By the early part of our review classes 31, 37 and 47 became well established remaining until the lines were electrified, when, in the late 1980s class 86 locomotives in push-pull mode with ex-Edinburgh-Glasgow driving trailers took over along with EMUs.

The Paddington to Worcester and Hereford service was another second-rank one in this category. Here the

InterCity makes the going easy.

The longer-distance routes radiating north and west from London are those which naturally come under this heading, together with the group of cross-country services centred on Birmingham, known as the North-East/South-West group although actually serving all Regions. They are the commercially important routes which have generally received preferential investment down the years.

The two foremost routes are the West and East Coast main lines to the North. On the West Coast route out of Euston, electric haulage became universal to the West Midlands, Liverpool and Manchester in the 1960s and later, to Glasgow from 1974 under the 'Electric Scots' banner. In the late 1980s the push-pull mode with purpose-built driving van trailers became widespread.

In contrast, the East Coast Main Line services from King's Cross to the West Riding, Newcastle and Edinburgh initially missed out on electrification, although as consolation it had its superlative 'Deltics' on principal services until 1978 when the HSTs were introduced. These reigned until commissioning of full electrification in the early 1990s and the arrival of class 91s working in push-pull mode with Mk 4 coaches and driving trailers.

On the Western Region, Inter-City services from London were principally marked by the provision of more powerful type 4 locomotives; 'Warship' and 'Western' diesel-hydraulics and the ubiquitous class 47s, with class 50s appearing from the mid '70s. The first production batch of HSTs entered service on Western Region routes to Bristol and

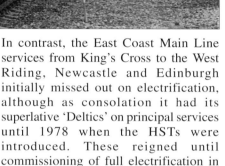

A particular trend of main line operations that became widespread over our 30 year review period was high speed push-pull working. An early example was the Edinburgh - Glasgow service which started in 1971 with pairs of adapted class 27 locomotives. This was superseded in 1979 by single 47/7s and driving trailers. Here a driving trailer is at the head of train as it arrives at Glasgow Queen Street in 1981.

Hymeks were mostly used in the early days whilst class 31s took over the medium-length trains of ubiquitous Mk 1s for a few years in the early 1970s. As HSTs were delivered on the major routes, displaced type 4 power and Mk 2 coaching stock became available and class 50s became much associated with the service.

Another route which the 50s were to make their own for ten years from 1980 was the old LSWR line from Waterloo to Exeter. Never actually designated an Inter-City route, the line eventually became something of an anomalous outpost of Network SouthEast. The preceding moderately powered class 33s had themselves taken over from the Warship hydraulics in 1971 and eight coach rakes were usual throughout.

Moving North and one particular strategic main line that has, until recently, been neglected by modellers is the Trans-Pennine route via Standedge (see photo). Perhaps the absence of a definitive model of the once synonymous class 124 Trans-Pennine unit has been a factor? However, locomotive passenger workings were commonplace throughout the 1970s with type 4 power in the guise of 40s and 46s on predominantly Mk 1 stock. By the 1980s, the route's moderate-length rakes of Mk 2s were noteworthy for providing some unusual last Deltic workings. After Sectorisation it was included with Provincial Services and received various builds of new Sprinter units. Short length, frequent interval passenger trains are now the norm.

Turning to main lines north of the Scottish border, the frequent Edinburgh-Glasgow run had its own class 126 Inter-City DMUs replaced in 1971 by a pioneering diesel push-pull arrangement. Six coach Mk 2 sets were 'top and tailed' by pairs of modified class 27s until superseded in 1979 with new class 47-powered sets made up from Mk 3 coaches and the first 'proper' driving trailers

The appeal of modelling the main Trans-Pennine route is surely enhanced by the countryside through which it runs; a splendidly contrasting mix of enchanting moorland scenery, dark satanic mills and crude enclaves of heavy industry. The Manchester Model Railway Society's 4mm 'Dewsbury Midland' layout, when running in 'blue diesel mode', successfully captures the flavour of the 1970s scene in this locality.

(converted from Mk 2 brake seconds) These Mk 3 sets also worked some fast services between Glasgow and Aberdeen, reminiscent perhaps of the last fling which some of Gresley's famous A4 Pacifics had on these expresses as late as 1966 - only 15 years earlier but under the banner of British Rail too!

Further North still and the Highland Main Line services to Inverness had been another very early dieselisation scheme. The celebrated pairings of class 24 and 26 locomotives gradually gave way in the mid 1970s to type 4 haulage, finally succumbing to the Super Sprinter revolution in 1990.

Interestingly, until the 1980s the Inverness workings were worked as separate portions to and from Edinburgh and Glasgow which were combined or split at Perth. Each of the portions, often still with Type 4 power, were run as short length expresses - an ideal prototype for space starved modellers of course. Another late survivor of this split train practice was the Lancashire to Scotland WCML service, with Liverpool and Manchester portions being combined at Preston and split again at Carstairs for Edinburgh and Glasgow.

This mention serves to remind us of similar services to and from London, which were generally uncommon in British Rail days but had been widespread in the steam era. One example was the midday Hull/Bradford to Kings Cross of

The practice of splitting trains en route for two separate destinations was not common in British Rail days, though some notable examples survived which make ideal subjects for modelling. The King's Cross to Hull/Bradford service was one such train that ran in the late 1970s, being split and rejoined at Doncaster. The Hull portion of the train, consisting typically of a 31 and four Mk 2ds, is seen here passing the sidings of the now closed RTZ plant at Melton early in 1978.

Coaching colours and Company stalwarts.

The classic Mk 1 coach served BR well and the cascading programme gave it many years of useful life on lesser duties. In its garb of corporate blue and grey, the livery in which more have appeared than any other, it constituted an enduring image of BR passenger travel for many years. The topic of coach liveries should not pass without comment, particularly some early colour variations.

The LMSR-inspired lined maroon livery had been the pre-1964 standard on Mk 1 stock and could just still be seen in secondary use as late as 1972/73. On the other hand, late surviving examples of the Southern Region's former standard green livery were not so common, although some transferred onto other Regions were seen running into 1970/71. In contrast, the Western Region's chocolate and cream, originally applied only to WR named trains, had very rare survivors lasting only until 1968.

The first Mk 2 FKs had actually appeared in maroon and green liveries, but being premium stock they were candidates for early repaints.

When the blue and grey livery became widespread, from about 1966/67, it should not be forgotten that in certain locations this gave the everyday opportunity for haulage by the last steam locomotives. The use of B1s and Fairburn tanks on the Leeds-Bradford leg of trains to Kings Cross is a well known example.

The most significant livery development for the modeller was the emergence of many new brands and liveries in the mid to late 1980s. The InterCity livery was the earliest to appear in 1983/84. Another well promoted at the time was the Scotrail identity; cascaded Mk 2 stock received a clever derivative of the InterCity livery. In retrospect, these developments were the harbinger of the myriad of colour schemes that have now appeared on the privatised system.

The early livery anachronisms serve as a reminder that some combinations of motive power and stock in the early part of our review period were equally curious. Passenger stock that was not exclusively of BR design ran regularly with diesel and electric locomotives. Whilst most pre-war stock, including the revered LNER Gresley vehicles, had virtually disappeared by 1964, examples of some other pre-nationalisation designs actually lasted a few years longer. This included LNER Thompson stock, SR Bulleid coaches, some repainted from green to maroon and transferred to the Eastern and Scottish Regions, and other notable survivors such as late Hawksworth GWR and Stanier LMS vehicles, a very few of which even received blue/grey livery.

These less usual conjunctions do offer the modeller of the early BR period the opportunity to include something unusual, although all such pre-BR designs of ordinary day coach had gone by 1971. Also the types and number details of those late survivors are vague, thus without further research, compromise or calculated liberties may be called for when modelling them. In contrast however, later survivors in specialised categories, including sleeping cars, Gresley and Thompson buffet cars (illustrated) and countless parcels vans are much more well recorded.

Ex-LNER Thompson buffet car No. Sc1706 in blue and grey. The 4mm model is built from a BSL kit by Ken Gibbons. The last of these various pre-nationalisation designs had gone by 1978.

the mid-1970s which saw short portions of Mk 2d air conditioned stock behind ETH fitted class 31/4s.

Others were the short type 4-hauled expresses which ran through the attractive settings of the Cornish main line, the catering vehicles having been detached at Plymouth for servicing.

Customer coaching

As we have seen, at the very start of our review period in 1964 the most commercially important routes were powered by nearly new locomotives and generally utilised the newer Mk 1 coaching stock on improved designs of bogie which were suitable for prolonged high speed running.

The first bulk introduction of integrally constructed Mk 2 stock occurred on the LMR electrified lines in 1965/66, and later builds provided stock of steadily improving quality.

In general funds for capital investment in new coaching stock were focused onto the highest-earning routes, and in consequence the established railway practice of 'cascading' became most marked during the 1970s.

Cascading involves the redistribution of coaching stock from the premium services, when displaced by newer builds, into use on the next lower levels of commercial operations. For example, when the ECML received its HST sets from 1978, the displaced Mk 2d air

conditioned stock found its way onto Midland Main Line and NE/SW services. This displaced Mk 2a vehicles (themselves earlier 'cascades' from the ECML in 1971) which were then available for the replacement of Mk 1s still in use elsewhere.

The complexity of the cascading programme is a research topic in itself and too convoluted for a detailed account here. Nevertheless, the principle means that with careful choice there are many opportunities to use premium service stock on layouts which portray railway locations away from the principal main lines. Note however, that only the first Mk 2 builds were fitted with vacuum brakes and thus could work with Mk 1s.

All subsequent Mk 2 and Mk 3 coach builds were fitted with air brakes and it was not uncommon for the later Mk 2 variants to run in mixed formations whether air-conditioned or not.

Developments in carriage heating occurred during the British Rail era too although the outwardly visible effects of significance to the modeller are generally subtle, involving only the correct choice of locomotive for a given set of stock. Typically, steam heated coaching stock dictates that diesel locomotives allocated to winter passenger duties should be fitted with steam heating boilers and feed water tanks. Likewise, air-conditioned stock requires an ETH fitted locomotive.

Before moving further down the pecking order of BR passenger workings, there are three more forms of express passenger train that need to be considered. We have called these Special Services, all of which, for various reasons have gradually become less relevant to rail travel patterns in Britain. They do however, deserve modest recognition in the annals of British Rail history and are thus outlined in further detail in the accompanying panel.

To summarise from a modelling point of view, the length of main line expresses in the classic mould generally renders them suited either to larger layouts or the smaller scales. Thankfully, there are many alternatives to the main line scenario which provide excellent modelling opportunities and these are considered next.

Special Services

Firstly, under this heading, the Motorail train, which allowed a car and its occupants to save a long drive en route to a holiday destination. The 1970s were the heyday of these services and most ran from London, or like the Stirling to Newton Abbott train, linked prime tourist areas. Motorails were heavy trains, with the passenger accommodation often being in surplus Mk 1 first class coaches and cars carried on Carflat wagons. Although only larger layouts would be able to portray them effectively, at the other end of the scale, a single GUV van could be used to provide limited car accommodation on winter or daytime trains. An example here was a late 1970s Newcastle-Bristol service which was otherwise composed of Mk 2 air conditioned stock with class 45/1 haulage

The second special service was the dedicated sleeper train service, for which Mk 1 sleeping cars were built in hundreds. Sleeper services mainly ran on routes from London to Scotland, the West and Wales, and also on the Scottish internal routes from Edinburgh and Glasgow to Inverness. Demand for stock, including the overnight Motorail trains, was even enough to keep some LNER, GWR and LMS sleeper designs operating into the 1970s. The eventual Mk 3 replacements were unusual in that they did not receive a specific regional allocation, rather they were worked as a pooled resource to cover the remaining services. However, sleeper traffic was falling off, due to ever shorter daytime journeys, and after only a few years many were stored out of use.

In 4mm scale at least, models of BR sleeping cars have been featured heavily. The long running Triang/Hornby Mk 1 coach range included a good example and the Mk 3 cars have been the subject of an excellent 4mm scale model by Lima.

Perhaps the most lamented sleeper service in BR days and relatively easy to adopt in model form is the London to Fort William service. This often consisted of just two through sleeper vehicles, although during the summer months it was increased to three or four depending on demand. In model form this service could easily be portrayed as a extra operational feature on a might-have-been Scottish outpost terminus station.

The last special services to be considered are the Pullman services, targeted at business travellers on the main routes into London.

Essentially a hangover from the glory days of steam, the increasing quality of ordinary stock made them something of an anachronism by the 1970s. The much admired Metro-Cammell built cars served the East Coast route until 1978, although the popular Western diesel units had gone in 1973.

Models of the East Coast cars are available in kit form in 4mm from Southern Pride, whilst the Blue Pullman vehicles from either the Triang or Kitmaster stables can occasionally be snapped up second-hand.

Provincial and Plebeian

From Cornwall to Caithness and Anglesey to Anglia, examination of cross-country, inter-urban and secondary routes reveals a legion of varied and interesting prototypes that generally can be adapted to smaller layout spaces. This is true of the whole period of our review, from the dismal days of grant aided neglect at the turn of the 1970s to the rejuvenation under the aegis of the Provincial Sector.

Although not exclusively, these secondary main lines and routes were the province of the humble DMU for many years. Whilst in their heyday the first generation units were much maligned, they have now acquired a definite cachet

of nostalgia and character and now, as if the wheel has turned full circle, DMU modelling is in vogue. They were the backbone of so many services on BR, especially through the '60s, '70s and early '80s, and are really quintessential for modellers of the British Rail era. Obviously a key point of 'multiple' units was to form longer formations when patronage demanded, and this is an occurrence not so often seen modelled.

Many of the second-generation class 140, 150 and 160 series DMU types have fortunately caught the attention of the proprietary manufacturers, the Heritage sets not so much, however. The late Colin Massingham, proprietor of Modern

Traction Kits, made valiant efforts to provide kits of all of the first generation types, including some in 2mm. The kits would not now sit well in today's more sophisticated market, however, in 4mm at least, the laurels must now go to DC Kits for showing that there is much latent modelling potential in these units.

The panel on page 95 gives a broad outline of the first generation DMU fleet and may give the impression that designs were developed for all eventualities. However, the fleet was soon affected by line closures and changing traffic patterns and many unit types ended up working services to which they were not ideally suited.

The Golden Valley line on the Western Region is typical of a 1970s cross-country route served by DMU stopping trains and through freight traffic. In 1979, 37102 threads through the valley with a mix of parcels vans, including a GWR Siphon G.

The reverse was true also; the 1969 transfer of a batch of class 120s from the Western to Etches Park depot at Derby proved to be more fitting than most DMU reallocations. Actually designated as 'Cross Country', the units provided very agreeable accommodation and were somewhat over specified for Western Region branches on which some had been used. During the 1970s the Derby based sets worked some long diagrams as a result of combining together local workings, such as from Lincoln to Nottingham and then on to Crewe, Matlock or Birmingham. They could be seen at Cleethorpes and Skegness, and also worked the Norwich and Cambridge to Birmingham services for some years before the reintroduction of locomotives and coaches.

The introduction of the class 150 Sprinters in 1985 displaced the 120s which then became part of the scene in Central Scotland and Ayrshire, and also on the North Wales and Manchester-Blackpool lines. (By this time many of the asbestos-insulated trailers had been replaced by those from class 101 units). Thus these versatile and far travelled units often assumed the role of a roaming

The class 120 Cross Country units operated on many provincial routes up until the mid '80s. Despite their versatility, no model is yet available either RTR or as a full kit. In 1978 a typical three car unit is seen entering Bangor, North Wales.

stop-gap, pending the provision of either locomotive haulage, Sprinters, or electrification. They are perhaps ideal prototypes for use on smaller cross country themed layouts. Unfortunately, as yet no ready to run model, or complete kit, of the 120 (or its close cousin the 119) exists in any scale, although one is pending from No Nonsense Kits at the time of writing.

There is of course equally rich potential in the many other designs of Heritage DMU, subject to the builder's preferences and ability in converting or kit-building. In the early years of the fleet some of the smaller batches were very parochial in their field of operation, and whilst allocations changed, no design can be considered a truly universal traveller, although by the last years of our review period the Metropolitan-Cammell class 101 would come close. Of the more numerous classes, the Birmingham RCW Co. 104 (the Hornby class 110 backdates fairly easily into an acceptable model), Cravens 105 and BR Derby 108 were seen over considerable areas of the London Midland, Eastern and North Eastern Regions. Modelling the variety of Heritage DMU (and EMU) types in 4mm scale has been much easier since the arrival of the DC Kits and Southern Pride ranges. Although not suited to outright beginners, these plastic kits build up into very good representations of the real thing. Moreover, fitting a drive mechanism is very straightforward, as illustrated in the panel overleaf.

An interesting interlude occurred with the DMU refurbishment programme which gained momentum through the 1970s and turned units out initially in a white livery with blue band. White was, of course, not a very practical colour and from 1978 onwards, refurbished sets were liveried in the standard blue and grey. The initial refurbished livery is often

Motorising a DMU/EMU kit from DC Kits.

The DC Kits range of plastic injection moulded kits of DMU and EMU prototypes are a boon to the British Rail era modeller. The kits go together well and the hardest part - that of motorising them - is now very straightforward thanks to the Antipodean Black Beetle drive unit.

1 All the DC Kits kits come with a standard floor moulding which is provided with a recessed hole for mounting the drive mechanism. The whole panel has to be removed to provide the necessary space and this can easily be cut out with a slitting disc.

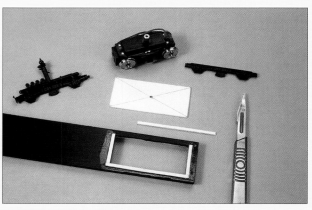

2 A new mounting plate is made up of 40 thou Plasticard which is 4mm larger all round than the hole in the floor. The moulded mounting spindle on the Black Beetle unit will slot through the central hole of the new mounting plate.

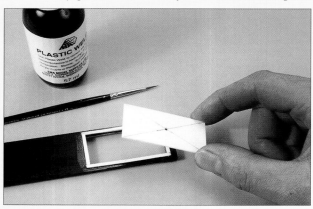

3 The spacing pieces are made from 4mm wide strips of 40 thou Plasticard and are fitted around the hole perimeter on the top side of the floor, as shown. These ensure that the mounting plate, when fitted, is located at the correct height.

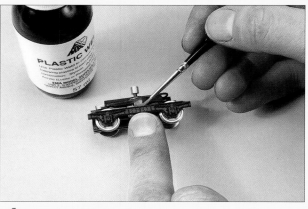

4 The Black Beetle unit is moulded with mounting lugs for attaching the bogie side frames included in the kit. Glue these in position with solvent taking care to ensure the axleboxes are correctly aligned. Finally fit the front and rear bogie stretchers.

5 Fitting the Black Beetle unit is so straightforward it doesn't really warrant this picture! Nevertheless, the motor unit spigot is pushed through the mounting hole and held in place by the brass nut leaving just a little 'slack' to allow it to pivot freely.

6 The finished item on a Cravens 105 unit. The Black Beetle is unobtrusive and cannot be seen at all through the unit's windows. One Black Beetle per two car unit appears to be sufficient. Fitting extra pick-ups on trailing bogies assists with current collection.

described as 'short lived', which is rather subjective of course, but misleading, since a few white cars survived into 1983/84 and can thus give a little more variety to a layout set in that period.

Classic Provincial Outposts

To round off our look at provincial and cross-country routes we consider those where the DMU has only relatively recently gained the hold that it has long held elsewhere. Comprehensive and well known instances of locomotive haulage in this connection, are the long, isolated routes of Northern and Western Scotland. On these routes, parcels traffic was always substantial until the 1980s and consequently locomotives, with their greater power and adhesive ability, were required to cope with the steeply graded lines. For many years these lines were worked by Type 2 diesels of various designs, the characterful Sulzer-engined classes 24, 25, 26 and 27 being the norm throughout the 1970s.

The routes fall basically into two groups; the former Highland Railway lines from Inverness to Wick and Thurso (the Far North line) and the Kyle of Lochalsh, and the old North British Railway route (the West Highland line) from Glasgow to Fort William and Mallaig. The virtues of these routes for modellers have been extolled many times. With short locomotive hauled trains of Mk 1 stock and parcel vans they make ideal prototypes for small layout themes.

An interesting operational phenomenon on both the Kyle line and Mallaig extension was the inclusion of goods stock on passenger trains. These operated as mixed trains in the old tradition, albeit with fully-fitted vacuum brakes. Examples of goods stock used on these trains range from the not-unexpected 12T Vanfit to 16T mineral wagons and even occasional Presflos.

The class 37 takeover on these routes in the early 1980s has been well documented, Scottish provincial services being the last bastion of steam heating until the ETH fitted class 37/4s arrived in 1985. Mk 2 stock was also in evidence by this time. Particularly reminiscent of this period were the large logo liveries with terrier and stag emblems and local names like 'Mary Queen of Scots' and 'Radio Highland'. The inevitable

'Sprinters', of class 156 arrived in 1989 displacing most of the locomotive hauled workings virtually overnight. Another route in the same mould worth modelling is the former Caledonian line to Oban which also supported notable freight traffic in the guise of timber and oil.

On many English and Welsh routes, there were always sporadic instances of medium length passenger workings with locomotive haulage on otherwise DMU-dominated routes. The small West Wales terminus of Milford Haven had some of its trains powered by boiler fitted class 37s, then wandering Southern Region class 33s, and later, Cardiff-based 37/4s. Other particularly memorable examples include the many summer Saturday trains to holiday destinations such as Skegness, Llandudno and Scarborough. The

inclusion of a summer special as a means of justifying an extra train has long been a tactic on countless terminus layouts!

Locomotive-hauled revival

As we hinted briefly in the opening paragraphs of this chapter, there was a resurgence of locomotive-hauled trains on many provincial and cross-country routes from the mid 1970s. This was aided by the cascading of stock from main line services, coupled with a surplus of type 2 and type 3 locomotives from changes in freight working.

As many of the first generation DMUs were now getting past their best, the availability of this reasonable quality Mk 1 and early Mk 2 stock allowed the displacement of the Inter City and Cross Country DMUs, which in turn enabled

Above. A secondary main line theme was used to good effect on Alan Lister's 00 gauge Haswell Moor layout. Set in the late '70s it catered for a variety of loco hauled and DMU passenger trains. The forlorn look of the rail scene at this time, as described in chapter 2, is also well portrayed in an usual winter setting.

Left. With the decline of freight and parcels traffic and the arrival of Sprinters in 1989 the Scottish provincial outposts became less obvious choices for modelling. However, the scenic attractions of these lines are still evident in this 1990 view taken at Clachnaharry.

Twilight of the Heritage sets.

During the late 1980s the Sprinter classes gradually took over the most commercially important Provincial Sector routes. The locomotive haulage revival was flagging and the remnants of the original DMU fleet suffered severe shortages due to poor serviceability and the early withdrawal of cars containing asbestos insulation.

One measure resorted to was the increased provision of 'power twins', by removal of trailers from three car sets. These could be 'hammered' into keeping time with Sprinter schedules.

More interesting for the modeller perhaps are the widespread transfers and reformations, with traditional Regional allegiances and the original distinctions between suburban, general purpose and Cross Country sets all becoming largely eroded. These changes were often on a very ad hoc and transient basis and resulted in types appearing in unprecedented locations and hybrid combinations. Examples include class 104 cars in Scotland and on Paddington suburban services, class 116, 117 and 119 power cars running in twin sets with class 101 vehicles, and 115s with 108s.

The newly styled Regional Railways applied a Sprinter style livery to some units in the early 1990s, but probably the most widely-applied Sector livery was that of Network SouthEast. This appeared on many cars including the refurbished 101s, 108s and 117s which had been forecast as being the last survivors of the heritage fleet, and some SR DEMUs. Naturally common in the Home Counties, it sometimes appeared in less obvious haunts such as Cornwall, Cheshire and even the North East.

Left. An unusual combination of a suburban 116 unit paired with a low density 114 unit is seen here in 1991 on a Scarborough-Leicester (SO) service approaching Beverley.
Right. Network SouthEast liveried class 101 unit (51208 and 54402) far from its 'home' territory is seen here at Hexham in 1988.

withdrawal of some of the less loved ordinary sets.

Although re-born loco haulage would again fade away ten or so years later with the coming of the Sprinters, the period proved to be very interesting and probably represents the zenith of the latter-day loco-hauled passenger network. As these services, in their locomotive-hauled incarnation, present very good potential for portrayal in model form we have set out details of a choice few in the panel opposite; Cross Country Classics worth modelling.

To support these services more examples of classes 31, 37 and 47 had to be converted to supply electric train heating. Moreover, the Southern Region's class 33s, farsightedly delivered with ETH equipment, were rostered for some quite extended diagrams in the 1980s. These took them as far afield as Crewe, Manchester and West Wales on a daily basis. Although vacuum braked Mk 1 and Mk 2 vehicles were principal players in this revival, some Mk 2 air braked variants, including air conditioned types, did later appear on Provincial Sector services, notably ScotRail Express routes. However, with the increased maintenance requirements of this stock, the prospect of shiny new Sprinters became the favoured option.

The Swinging Seventies?

Most classic DMU-operated routes had a requirement to convey parcels or mail traffic which was greater than the capacity of the units' van space. From early days a practice developed of attaching a parcels van to the DMU as tail traffic, subject to the power-to-weight ratio of the hauling unit. This became euphemistically know as a 'swinger' and the practice was once widespread, even examples of a milk tank and a fish van having been photographed. The last known parcels van 'swinger' is thought to have been operated around 1980. This makes an interesting sideline for a layout where the vehicle could even be shunted by the DMU itself.

Where there was more parcels traffic than a swinger could handle, one or two daily trains would be formed of several Mk 1 coaches and a selection of parcels vans. The Exeter-Barnstaple route, as portrayed on our featured

layout Lapford Road, is one example which lasted into the early 1980s. Slightly earlier examples, from the 1970s, included the Newcastle-Carlisle, the Worcester to Birmingham and the York-Hull routes.

Cross-Country Classics worth modelling

All of these cross-country routes embody in one package so many of the overlooked virtues of the British Rail era. They traverse sequences of urban, industrial and rural scenery and, in the late 1970s and early 1980s, witnessed short locomotive-hauled formations running alongside Speedlink style freight traffic. Moreover, the routes were abound with traditional infrastructure, Company vernacular buildings and signalling.

When locomotive-hauled, six coaches would be typical on most services. There would be at least one brake vehicle, and a minimum half-coach of first class accommodation. For a compact layout, representative four-coach rakes, not necessarily in these set orders, could be:

BSK/CK/TSO/TSO

BSO/FK/TSO/TSO

BFK/TSO/TSO/TSO

All vehicles could be Mk 1 or Mk 2 vacuum-braked, apart from the CK, and a Mk 1 SK would be regarded as an equivalent to a TSO. A longer rake could be formed by adding another TSO or SK, or another option would be to add a BSO(T) micro-buffet or a BG van.

Cardiff-Bristol-Salisbury-Portsmouth
Used class 123 Inter-City DMUs until 1968 when class 35 Hymeks took over with Mk 1 rakes including an RMB. From 1972 a mix of WR Cross Country and SR 3H diesel-electric MU sets. Class 31 haulage came in from 1977, followed by the 33s.

Cardiff-Hereford-Shrewsbury-Crewe
Formerly an important route whose long-distance trains were diverted via Birmingham from 1970. Worked by six-

For a few years before Sprinters appeared, the Hull-Sheffield-Manchester service saw 31/4s on four coach rakes. An eastbound service is seen here near North Ferriby in 1986.

car Cross Country DMUs, usually strengthened with a class 121 Bubble Car. A brief use of the 123 Inter-City sets was followed in 1977 by boiler-fitted class 25s. From 1981 SR class 33s worked on detached diagrams, and from 1986, Cardiff-allocated class 37/4s.

Norwich-Peterborough-Leicester-Birmingham
Made up from a sequence of local services when another cross-country line closed in 1966. A mix of general purpose and Cross Country DMUs gave way to Mk 1 locomotive-hauled stock in 1977, consistently rostered for class 31s and later 31/4s.

Hull-Sheffield-Manchester
The 1979 'South Trans-Pennine' service, tied in with the recast of that over the Northern route, was a revival of a pre-

1960s service pattern. A fleet of hybrid class 123/124 Inter-City DMUs, which were withdrawn wholesale in 1984, were replaced by 31/4s; coaching stock was unusually short formations of four Mk 2s, with odd Mk 1 substitutions.

Aberdeen-Inverness
A specific build of class 120 Cross Country sets were unique to this line until 1980, when they were replaced by classes 26 and 27 on mixed Mk 1/Mk 2 rakes. Typical mid-1980s provision was class 47/4s in Scotrail livery, with class 37 substitutions

Glasgow-Ayr-Stranraer
Services operated in connection with the steamers to Larne in Northern Ireland. The class 126 Inter-City DMUs, run as an extension of the Ayr service, were withdrawn in 1981 and replaced by haulage with class 27s. By 1984 class 47s were working unique red and blue 'Sealink' Mk 1 stock, followed by ScotRail-liveried Mk 2s.

Commuterland

The South East, London, and beyond
We take our heading for this section by paraphrasing the name of the Sector which would eventually become Network SouthEast. Far from being bland, standardised or uninteresting, the myriad of electric multiple unit types which form the backbone of Southern passenger operations actually provides an exacting challenge for dedicated rolling stock modellers and those whose partiality is for concentrated operation would have to search hard for something more

intensive. A particular angle here could be to develop a home based multiple circuit layout on several levels with automatic train control and state of the art cityscape scenic modelling - indeed a diametric antithesis of the little shunting layouts many of us seem to drool over. Certainly South London is brimming with just such prototypes where railway tracks, either perched on lofty viaducts or submerged in deep cuttings, interlace with each other amongst high rise office buildings.

Equally though, the idyllic approach is also perfectly valid for the Southern Electric patch, and some notable layouts on the exhibition circuit, such as Nigel Bowyer's Elm Park, Graham Clark's Effingham South, have illustrated the concept well. Essentially these are third-rail versions of the classic branch line.

Generally, Southern EMUs were built in two or four car units, and of three categories: main line or suburban, or stock for country districts which was of suburban pattern but with toilets. Pre-war

Early British Rail on the Southern Region is exquisitely depicted on Hull Miniature Railway Society's Chessington Chalk Lane, a supposed commuter line terminus which incorporates some MOD sidings to add operational interest.

units in all three categories ran into the blue livery era, including the famous Brighton Belle sets. British Railways EMU construction followed the same standards as contemporary hauled stock, particularly the BR Mk 1 coach, until the many sliding door units introduced from the 1970s spread onto various services. The first radically new main line units were the stylish Wessex Express units of the late 1980s.

The main lines to Kent, the South Coast and Bournemouth have been included in this heading, as these are still moderate distances by national standards and have utilised EMUs on virtually all passenger workings during the review period. Traditional formations could include up to twelve cars, with many services programmed to 'split' en route to serve alternative destinations. As with DMUs, this presents operating potential which is very rarely seen modelled.

Network SouthEast, when it came into being, had the remit to include service workings north and west of London within a given radius, many having been early conversions to overhead electric traction. Undoubtedly the most visible element of the Sector from 1986 has been its extremely distinctive red, white and blue striped livery. It was a particular contrast after

Dave Seymour's large exhibition layout, Ashleigh, portrays aspects of the Southern electric network in the late BR period when the Network SouthEast livery predominated.

the brief appearance of a much more subtle brown and orange livery, dubbed 'Jaffa cake', on some refurbished EMUs, but in the changeover period many coaches carried a more discreet overbranding on the blue and grey.

Our 'commuterland' category should not, of course, be restricted to London and the South East. Many other major provincial conurbations in the UK have similar, albeit smaller, networks of commuter style operations, mostly coming under the umbrella of the various Passenger Transport Executives from around 1970. Certain provincial electrifications, such as Manchester to Bury and those within the Liverpool area, had actually been very long established, but other urban networks, such as in West Yorkshire, only finally became electrified

well into the British Rail era. Whereas some received brand new electric stock of the second generation, others had to use EMUs seconded from elsewhere.

Obviously all of the PTE services were ripe candidates for receiving their own identities. Starting with some of the earliest refurbished DMUs in the white and blue livery, all of the PTEs applied their own logos to BR stock which they subsidised for use in their areas. Naturally in time this manifested itself into full scale new liveries, which most PTEs limited to EMUs and second-generation DMUs. The bold Strathclyde orange-red and black was the only one applied in quantity to Heritage DMUs, and some PTEs have only reliveried odd units for trial or promotional purposes.

We have already commented on the how the Southern networks provide the ideal prototype for the operational enthusiast with the desire to recreate something of Clapham Junction. A current example of this is Paul Wade's Tonbridge West Yard. Even for the keen modeller of such units though, the favoured option is probably to build a layout which includes some form of freight activity. An early and mould breaking example in this genre was Terry Onslow's Witton layout which was a third rail branch terminus with a pair of freight exchange sidings at the back serving an offstage industrial estate. This particular layout from the mid 1980s was the

inspiration behind our layout scheme Eastoke, which is detailed below.

The scheme examines, through a fictitious approach, a quieter backwater of commuterland which includes a possible freight theme. Another angle might be a 1970s or 1980s layout depicting delivery of roadstone from the Mendips, a specific bulk traffic which is particularly associated with the Home Counties and was depicted on Dave Seymour's Ashleigh layout.

Commuter corridor railways now, more than ever before, offer huge scope for modelling and particularly so for those enthusiasts who find appeal in the multiplicity of colourful liveries or in intensive operation. At one time the main problem in representing such a system was once again in the availability of the necessary multiple-unit stock, but thankfully the situation is now changing, at least in 4mm scale. Both Hornby and Bachmann are producing new generation examples and several specialist manufacturers are regaining ground with kits of older electric units.

Eastoke

It is an indisputable fact that the electrified lines on the Southern Region were hardly affected by the closures of the mid-sixties. One line that was closed however was the Hayling Island branch. Despite buoyant passenger figures, it never gained the protective cloak of electrification. Here, we have supposed that it did happen along with an extension of the line to the south east corner of the Island, to Eastoke in fact which also includes a track down to a small port at Eastoke Quay.

Passenger services would have been solely in the hands of 2HAP units from the early 1970s with the occasional visit from a 4VEP. Prior to this, the last survivors of the Southern Railway's fleet, 2 BILs and 4 CORs, could be seen. Generally, the 2 car units would use the bay platform alone.

As for freight, the goods yard at Hayling is assumed to have coped with the Islands needs beyond 1940 when Eastoke's own yard was converted to deal with fuel and oil deliveries to an MOD tank farm. After 1945, the facility slipped out of use until the 1950s when coastal tankers took advantage of Eastoke's position and facilities. Now owned by the Eastoke Tank Storage Co., most of the products handled (petrol, fuel oil, etc), are bound for the Channel Islands.

Class 33s or 73s arrive from Fawley with nine 45t 4-wheel tankers and run into the loop, which, like the rest of the yard, is non-electrified. The loco runs around, buffers up and propels the tanks a short way into the headshunt to collect one of the two 'propelling' brake vans stationed here. The assembled train is then shunted under the control of the brake van into the empty siding. The empty tankers are then collected but, prior to setting off for Fawley, the second propelling brake van is detached in the headshunt, for the next incoming train to use.

The layout itself is suitable for a garage, or along one wall of a hobby room.

The boards could be of traditional timber and board construction, as the scenery in this part of the Island is relatively flat. That said, it would be beneficial to raise the trackbed by half an inch or so above the main board, using fibreboard. This would allow part of the area to the front of the layout to gently fall away from track level, suggesting a site near to the coast.

Eastoke at a glance
Location; Hayling Island, Hampshire.
Period; 1970 - 1985.
Suggested scale; 4mm - 1foot.
Size of Layout; 3.96m x 0.60m (13ft x 2ft)
Locomotive classes; 33, 73
Multiple units; 2HAP (cl. 414).
Typical rail traffics; EMU service to Havant, Oil traffic from Fawley. Occasional through freight traffic to Eastoke Quay could include spot traffic for import/export, such as grain or palletised commodities.

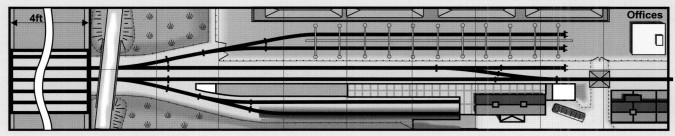

Branches still hanging

At the very start of the British Rail era, the quaint old branch passenger set with its attendant tank locomotive was close to extinction. The last of the push-pull workings bowed out during 1965 and probably the last steam worked branch in the classic mould was that through the New Forest from Brockenhurst to Lymington Pier, electrified along with the Bournemouth main line in 1967.

The closure of countless branch lines is most closely associated with Dr Beeching, but despite the excesses of his era, numerous branches still survived, albeit in rationalised form. However, the term 'branch line' was by this time becoming something of a misnomer. The traditional concept of a branch line; that of a sleepy single track railway threading its way through leafy glades to a picturesque terminus, as exemplified by all those models of Ashburton, had, more or less perished forever. There were a few exalted examples, of course, like St Ives, Looe, Falmouth, Barton-upon-Humber, Windermere, all of which eluded the grip of the good Doctor to survive until the present day, and others such as Alston, Swanage and Bridport which cheated him only until the 1970s.

By the early years of the blue period many of the so called branches still extant had been important main lines in better days. Examples include that from Birkenhead to Chester which had once carried Paddington-bound expresses, and the Bedford-Bletchley line, which before 1968, had been part of an important cross country artery linking Cambridge and Oxford and carrying a mix of DMU passenger and inter-Regional freight and parcels services.

By supposing that the old patterns of working on lines like these had survived ten, or even twenty years, the routes become ideal candidates for interesting layout themes.

Other branches that survived were actually truncated, basic remnants of former important cross country routes. Examples include Matlock on the Midland main line through the Peak District, llkley, Colne, Keswick, and East Grinstead. In some of these cases too, the lines beyond still continued for freight traffic, such as the North Warwickshire line from Birmingham to Stratford-upon-Avon. This line once formed part of the GWR route to South Wales and the West Country and for a few years the line south of Stratford station was retained as a freight route avoiding the Lickey Incline. Others in this genre were at Blaenau Ffestiniog (to Trawsfynydd nuclear power station), Okehampton in Devon (where the line to Meldon Quarry still runs through), and at Bishop Auckland (bypassing the station en route to the Blue Circle works at Eastgate). In some ways our featured layout, New Quay, has adopted this prototype approach on a

smallish scale. More ambitious modellers with a tad more space could develop the theme to include substantial through freight operations.

Many secondary and provincial routes which had not been artificially foreshortened found themselves demoted in status too, although often this was more a result of the creeping rationalisation process. The Cambrian Coast route, once the pride of the pre-group company, was little more than a very long branch by this time. The Hull to Scarborough line is another example where singling of track, coupled with minimal investment and the slow decline of services gave this once senior route a definite ambience of 'branch line syndrome'. The Exeter to Barnstaple route is another case in point. Curiously, both of these routes quite independently engendered two of our featured layouts in this book.

Lapford Road (below) and Reighton (opposite) are both examples of how this prototype theme was developed using some careful modellers' licence to include additional freight activity.

Having taken it upon ourselves to redefine one of the hobby's most sacred doctrines, this latter-day branch line concept is one which we proclaim can be unexpectedly inspiring and readily adopted for smaller space layouts. Furthermore, whilst it was a noticeable

outcome of the Beeching era changes that surviving branches frequently lasted either for passenger or freight usage, but rarely for both, in our virtual modeller's world, this fact can be neatly side stepped to open up a wide choice of freight commodities that could be run.

These are the vital extra ingredients for sustaining operating interest - unless you really do just want to model a branch passenger station on a thin plank of wood - and a selection are explored more thoroughly in the freight chapters.

Offshoots on the branch.
Whatever branch line theme you choose, the archetypal blue period branch passenger train is a DMU set appropriate to the region of choice. This is the direct operational equivalent of the local or push-pull set which would be a standard part of the roster on a steam period branch layout. The Modernisation Plan and second-generation fleets have been given some consideration already, but there are certain offshoots of both which are particularly apposite for branch line working and which deserve examination before closing this chapter.

Surviving into the early years of our review period was a selection of experimental four-wheel railbuses, after a fashion popular on the Continent.

Unfortunately, the British application of these vehicles generally failed and all

Above. The original station at Bishop Auckland was still used as a terminus in this 1979 shot. The freight line to Eastgate branched off immediately before the platform. Now, only a 'basic bus shelter' platform exists alongside the former freight line. Below and opposite. The diesel branch line scene epitomised in 1982 by Lapford Road (left) and in 1983 by Reighton (right).

were withdrawn by 1968 with none carrying Rail Blue livery. The railbus era was nevertheless an interesting interlude and one which provides countrywide inspiration for small diesel age branch line themes in the early part of the British Rail era.

For example, one could assume that passenger workings on the Speyside line survived a year or two longer, operating alongside green and early blue class 20, 24 and 26 on whisky traffic. Certainly the vehicles make very attractive models, the Park Royal design being probably the most well-known due to the Airfix/Dapol 4mm scale kit.

Perhaps the best known offshoot occurred as a result of the Western Region's individualistic policy towards its Modernisation Plan DMU orders. These included two batches of single motor brake vehicles, later given TOPS class numbers 121 and 122 but much better known as the infamous 'Bubble Cars'. Although of the suburban

bodystyle, these were inherently suited to branch line operation as well as main line stopping services, and probably seen as natural successors to the GWR AEC railcars. Despite the obvious suitability of the concept, no other Modernisation Plan units were designed in this format.

The 121s remained almost exclusively on the Western Region throughout most of our review, and virtually any Western branch line-themed layout could support one. They were included in the refurbishment programme and appeared in both Blue and Grey and Network SouthEast liveries. The obvious Cornish applications include Falmouth, Newquay, and the much-vaunted Looe branch which has spawned many a layout plan over the years. As suggested earlier, branches closed in the mid-1960s could conceivably be 'reprieved' by the modeller, and such applications for a 'Bubble Car' are in ex-Southern Railway territory at places such as Lyme Regis and Seaton. Longer surviving examples include; Bristol-Severn Beach, Cardiff-Penarth, Slough-Windsor, the Bourne End-Marlow branch, and of a more urban nature, the West Ealing-Greenford shuttle service.

Line closures eroded much of the natural territory of the Western single cars, but their versatility stood them in good stead and they were often mixed into

conventional formations. Many also found departmental use, especially as route-learning cars. The slightly older 122s were earlier to leave the Western and became quite dispersed in later years. The batch at Tyseley had actually switched to London Midland management by dint of boundary changes, but carried on in the same West Midlands services, most notably the intensive Stourbridge Town shuttle. This urban Black Country branch had freight traffic in the 1960s, and a model interpretation could develop this for a slightly later period, perhaps servicing a small foundry or canal wharf. Other more rural uses for the Tyseley units included the Severn Valley line in its BR days, and between Leamington Spa and Stratford-upon-Avon.

However, once the 'Bubble Cars' had found their way onto another Region's allocation, they could be sent to other suitable locations, leaving the way clear for the imaginative modeller to find other plausible uses. In 1972 one was transferred south for the Watford-St Albans branch and in the 1980s they could be found on the experimental Kettering-Corby service and the Stockport-Stalybridge shuttle. Thus an LMR 'bubble car' would certainly not be out of place anywhere in the East, West or South Midlands.

Some early 122 transfers to Scotland had been intended as railbus replacements, but in the event found various uses, including conversions for parcels traffic. The modeller could likewise find various applications north of the Border, but the Eastern Region, alas, never found any outlets for their particular talents.

4mm scale modellers have for many years carried out a conversion on the Lima class 117 to produce a 'Bubble car', but the firm have recently introduced one themselves and a kit is available in 7mm. As we have shown, layout applications for these units are almost as geographically dispersed, and certainly more chronologically varied than for the earlier railbuses.

New buds on the branch

A key element of the strategy for the replacement of such 'Heritage' DMUs in the mid 1980s was the four wheeled 140

Above. The last-built Class 121 'Bubble Car' W55035 drops two passengers at Toller on the Maiden Newton - Bridport Branch in September 1972.

Right. Railbuses of AC and Park Royal builds at Grangemouth in June 1967. Such units are useful for selected Western, Scottish or Eastern region branch layouts prior to 1968. 4mm kits of at least three prototypes have seen production over the years.

series of second-generation units, branded as 'Pacers' by the marketing men. The Hornby model of the class 142 is an excellent product and a kit is also available in 7mm scale. This modern railbus is very suited to late BR era branch line themes, but is predominantly a North Country type. A small batch in GWR-style brown and cream livery, styled as 'Skippers', did work in Devon and Cornwall on first introduction but their lightweight construction was not ideally suited to conditions on some of the branches. A few well-publicised fiascos saw them transferred North, still wearing their devolutionary livery for some time.

The second generation equivalent of the 'Bubble Car' is the class 153 single unit which resulted partly from the shortcomings of the 142s. Provincial's conversion of these from two car class 155 Sprinters began in 1991 and the units have spread far and wide, including turns in Lincolnshire, North Wales, Cumbria

and the West Country. A conversion kit is currently available to adapt the ex-Dapol 4mm scale model of the 155.

At the other end of the spectrum it should be mentioned that there are certain stations under our broad branch theme which have attracted investment in electrification. Lymington Pier, already mentioned, and others on the overhead system, such as St Albans Abbey and Braintree, may possibly be rather too close to the old archetype of the 'bus sheltered basic railway', but other locations provide attractive prototypes, like the terminus at Lanark, which still had some traditional freight traffic until 1983 at least.

So there we have, in almost a nutshell, an exposé and summary of many aspects of British Rail era passenger activity. Hopefully, the double edged myth of insufficient interest and lack of variety has been dispelled forever.

Now for even more interesting bits.....

Chapter Four
Rail Freight in Transition

Our thirty year review period saw wide ranging changes to freight services on Britain's railways. Whilst the motive power revolution, initiated by the Modernisation Plan, was well established by the early 1960s, the changes in freight activity started slightly later and followed more of an evolutionary course. This encompassed changes in operating practices, increased train speeds and mould breaking developments in the wagon fleet which at last made the British railway wagon something that could stand comparison with its Continental counterparts rather than its Victorian predecessors.

Moreover, there were major shifts in the nature of commodities carried which led to the demise of archetypal station goods yards and the rise of often highly specialised bulk handling terminals.

Throughout these freight chapters we make use of terms such as 'traditional period' and 'Speedlink era' to denote particular historical spans. However, it must be emphasised that it is not possible to precisely define such periods; as indeed with the preceding coverage of passenger operations, some of the distinctions to be drawn are based more on traffic flows, available vehicles and working methods. New developments were sometimes introduced on an ad hoc basis, and whilst they may have appeared unplanned when considered in isolation, the many distinct and individual threads are inextricably interwoven into an overall gradual transition. This presents an endlessly fascinating range of possibilities for the modeller of the British Rail era as we shall now explore.

Block trains in vogue
With little serious competition from other modes, railway freight operations prior to 1939 had been predominantly geared to moving an incredible diversity of loads between an almost infinite variety of points. These included thousands of railway owned facilities as well as many privately owned sidings. After the war, road haulage began to gain considerable ground in many areas of domestic freight movement, yet despite this, the 1955

Modernisation Plan aimed to commit further resources into the railway's established methods of working as a matter of policy.

Faster transit times for 'wagonload' general merchandise, a priority before the war, became a prime objective and by the early part of our period, an extensive programme of fitting wagons with vacuum brakes had taken place along with considerable investment in automated marshalling yards. Palletisation and containerisation also became solutions in some spheres and appropriate wagon designs, such as the 'Palvans', appeared.

However, these measures were too late, the reducing restrictions on the road haulage sector, coupled with the expanding road network, led to increasing loss of traffic. Thus at the start of our review period the conventional wagonload unit was increasingly being seen as a thing of the past and in an attempt to rationalise operating costs, the new thinking in vogue, became block, or trainload, working of freight trains.

To quote a later BR chairman, Sir Peter Parker, rail freight had always been "basic to the basic industries" and the movement of coal - the original block rail freight commodity - was perhaps the most basic of all. Although there had been

block industrial coal trains formed of high capacity wagons for some time, the early British Rail years saw the introduction of the 'Merry-go-round' concept of operation between modern mechanised pits and the then new generation of high output power stations.

The steel industry was also in the throes of reorganisation at this time and semi-finished steel products, particularly between Scunthorpe and South Wales, became another high profile block traffic in the 1960s.

At this time these traffics, associated with other nationalised industries, still used wagon stock provided by BR. Few customers provided their own, but the oil companies were however an exception. They had long operated sizeable fleets of tank cars and the increased oil production of the period threw the spotlight on the benefits of privately owned or hired wagon fleets, leading subsequently to the resurgence of the privately owned wagon.

Car production was a boom industry in the 1960s and cars themselves, as well

Twilight of the pick-ups: Ex-works blue Clayton No. D8529 is seen with 21t coal hoppers at Kirkby Stephen West in April 1968. This attractive Type 1 class has been available as a Dave Alexander 4mm kit for some years, however, speculation of a model from Bachmann will hopefully prompt a growth of 1960s based layouts portraying the surviving remnants of the pick-up scene in Northern Britain.

as their components, became increasingly carried by rail, almost always in block train format. The corresponding increase in trunk road building at the dawn of the 1970s also fuelled a growth in rail borne aggregates traffic. This was another notable early example of private rail wagon investment.

In respect of these trainload workings it could be said that the words 'block' and 'bulk' were synonymous with trains moving between one private siding and another. However, the drive towards block working also sought to combine the common mileage of other commodities moved in smaller quantities and in traditional pattern wagons. One example was the marshalling together of short cuts of wagons from several adjacent collieries into a block train destined for a coal concentration depot.

Block trains apart, improving the viability of non-trainload flows was still a priority and it became a key aim of the National Freight Train Plan of 1966. However, this focused chiefly on the cutting of operating costs and any major expansion in the activity was not seen as an option. In 1968 the carriage of 'sundries' (i.e. less than full wagon loads which were grouped together in one vehicle for related destinations) came within the remit of the newly formed National Freight Corporation and its operational arm, National Carriers Ltd. Although the NFC was a wholly owned subsidiary of the British Railways Board,

ironically, it was under no obligation to actually use rail transport!

So it was against this backdrop that the old wagonload network and its related operating practices limped into the 1970s.

The Air Braked Network and Speedlink

Within a few years, however, it was realised in some quarters that even the cost effective block train operations would not sustain sufficient long term income on account of the generally low haulage charging rates prevailing in the bulk haulage market. In contrast, the distribution sector's cargoes of consumer goods were commanding premium rates and thus thoughts once again turned towards the concept of wagonload operation, albeit with a more clearly defined network after the manner of the Inter-City passenger system.

After some pilot running of the first batches of air braked vans, notably with Kelloggs' products from Trafford Park, the early 1970s saw the introduction of the Air Braked Network. This was essentially the precursor of what would ultimately become 'Speedlink'. The fundamental principle of this new initiative was the overnight operation of trunk freight trains composed of a limited number of cuts of wagons - effectively 'mini' block workings from various sources combined into one train for the common part of their journey. This

discipline was intended to radically cut down on intermediate remarshalling and provide the customer with a much quicker 'next day' delivery.

The first ABN service from Bristol to Glasgow started in October 1972. Unfortunately, with all the accompanying hassles of transhipment at either end, it was not an immediate success. The Harwich-Glasgow service a year later was however a step nearer to the total distribution package which was expected by the target market. The train ferry from Zeebrugge was a key link in that service and many commodities and goods were conveyed in large air braked 'ferry' wagons from European railways. BR, at the time, possessed only a few such vehicles of its own, but nevertheless, the complete transition in the UK to high capacity air braked freight wagons had now begun.

Concurrent with this initiative was the start of a renewed emphasis on serving private sidings. BR was glad to be able to rid itself of the archetypal public goods sidings that had been provided at all stations since Victorian times. The new freight sidings which began to spring up were radically different in format. They were owned by private companies providing break-bulk and warehousing services or road/rail transhipment facilities. Aided by the contemporary availability of Section 8 grants in the mid 1970s, many of these sidings subsequently became a cornerstone of Speedlink. Increased investment in new general purpose vans and opens occurred at this time too, providing BR with wagons like the VDA vans and OBA opens. In 1977 the new network officially acquired the brand name of 'Speedlink', being launched by Sir Peter Parker with a bottle of Guinness stout, a much prized traffic of the new service. From its inception it continued to expand, mainly by way of running more trains to increase capacity on the main routes, and by 1984 virtually all surviving classic wagonload traffic had

Left. The rail freight scene in 1990 provides a strong contrast to that illustrated on the previous page. High capacity bogie vans and steel carriers are much in evidence here at Warrington Dallam in April 1990. Nothing of the 'traditional' railway can be seen, the only covered accommodation being a Portacabin site office. A fork lift truck and mobile crane effect loading and unloading.

Freight sidings in the Speedlink period.

Left. The Stockton Haulage depot at Stranrear, seen here with 08 727 on 25/07/85, is an example of the type of rail freight yard that appeared in the 1970s and 1980s. The covered loading area and gantry crane can easily be modelled using embossed plastic sheet and Plastruct. Vans, open wagons and containers would predominate, but other non-bulk rail traffics could also be justified.

Left. An example of an even simpler freight facility is the Isis Link steel siding at Orb in South Wales. With just a modern gantry crane and hardstanding, the concept can be easily applied on the smallest of layouts and for numerous commodities.

Below. Not all depots served by Speedlink services were of new construction, as this shot of St Peter's scrapyard at Byker illustrates.

Below. The air braked equivalent of the traditional mixed freight train is epitomised by this Speedlink trunk haul service behind 31 278 at Leamside on the 21/10/86. Oil and coal wagons are most numerous, but also conveyed are single examples of cement and grain wagons and one VGA van.

officially been transferred onto the new network. The decade was probably the heyday of Speedlink with well known and well publicised carryings including Taunton Cider, Rowntrees chocolate from York, Campbells soup, large rolls of newsprint from Corpach and newly imported Renault cars.

From the modeller's point of view a Speedlink trunk haul train is probably the BR era equivalent of the traditional mixed freight from the steam age. Train consists were also further increased with smaller air braked block flows which had predated Speedlink, such as the chemical flows between Hull (Saltend) and Baglan Bay, and also included fuel oil in 45T tank cars for BR diesel depots. Even the engineers' departments acquired seconded air braked wagons, marked with their prefixes for the carriage of priority stores.

The Sub-Sector Effect.

With the introduction of Sectorisation, the Railfreight sector became divided up into six management divisions, although as far as outward appearances were concerned, nothing much changed apart from the appearance of the overall grey livery with red solebar stripe and large double arrow logo, first seen in 1982 on the new class 58s. This clearly marked out, in theory at least, the Sector's own allocation of dedicated locomotives.

Of the six divisions, five dealt with bulk commodities, which were largely handled by block train methods, these being Coal, Construction, Metals and Automotive, Petroleum and Chemicals and Industrial Minerals. The final division (which later became called Railfreight Distribution) covered general merchandise and edible products and was a wide ranging umbrella of mainly wagonload carryings which were the very stuff of Speedlink.

As mentioned briefly in chapter one, in late 1987 these management divisions became stand alone business units under the sub-Sector structure and the Railfreight image was radically relaunched with a new overall 'triple grey' locomotive livery which could be overlaid with a range of insignia for each business sub-Sector as appropriate.

However, the distinct identity that each sub-Sector was gaining was down

The decline of traditional freight working.

Although the underlying trend of the main narrative is generally positive and upbeat, overlaid and concurrent with the developments therein was the steady decline of the old ways of working.

At the start of our review, surviving steam traction was now increasingly restricted to freight traffic and once proud passenger Pacifics, together with types like Stanier Jubilees and Gresley V2s, could be seen hauling freights both fast and slow. Of course, steam soon became extinct as a matter of policy, but it was closely followed by the premature withdrawal of many new diesel types too. Reasons were numerous, but notably, the time honoured pick up goods train, to which the low powered types were suited, was in terminal decline at this time.

Perishable goods traffics connected with the food chain disappeared in droves. These were obvious targets in the 1960s for faster, versatile and more reliable road transport and BR's fleets of specialised vans and containers for meat, fruit, fish and frozen food were decimated by the end of the decade. There were a few notable survivors which, although untypical, lend themselves to adoption by modellers. Cattle traffic under early diesel haulage became generally unknown except for a few rare services to and from ports and harbours. Milk trains ran from the West Country until 1980 (see page 86) whilst another notable late survivor in the perishable category was fish from Wick, brought south in 'Blue Spot' vans attached to passenger trains until 1981.

With the traditional wagon fleet itself, the decline initially began with the progressive elimination of unfitted vehicles. By our 1964 starting point the fleets of general merchandise vans and opens were effectively fully vacuum fitted, but within a few years even vehicles of very recent construction were finding themselves increasingly redundant. Although the technically superior air brake gradually took over on most of the more commercially important flows, the vacuum brake did persist for many years, even on new and rebuilt wagons, and has still not been totally eliminated today.

Considering the eagerness of the 1955 Modernisation Plan to bring an end to the unfitted wagon, it still survived until the end of our review period, albeit in increasingly isolated pockets. The Southern Region and the north of Scotland had been first to completely eliminate unfitted trains in 1977.

Unfitted steel carrying vehicles were thinned out by the early years of full dieselisation but traditional coal carrying wagons remained as the major fleet without automatic brakes. They lingered largely because of outdated transhipment facilities at collieries and ports on old established traffic flows. Thus, even with Merry-go-round working having an overwhelming impact, unfitted mineral wagons could still be seen well into the 1980s, the very last being the carriage of Welsh coal to Swansea docks for export to Ireland in well worn 21T vehicles.

Other unfitted vehicles hung on in small fleets through the 1970s, examples including the carriage of grain and UK mined iron ore, which was in a state of terminal decline anyway. Unfitted examples of the civil engineers' Grampus spoil wagons outlasted revenue earning stock by some years.

The last two unfitted freight workings in 1994 both actually involved privately owned vehicles on very localised mineral workings around Blyth and Grimsby. This was quite fitting really, and ironic in the extreme, in view of the way that the concept of the private owner freight wagon had changed out of all recognition since the 1960s.

This example of the standard vacuum braked BR 12T van dates from the mid 1950s, but, as described in the main text, even those built as recently as 1962 soon found themselves redundandant. Their limited capacities, short wheelbases and primitive suspensions being unsuited to the new bulk load, high speed culture that was steadily emerging.

The model was built by Ian Fleming utilising a Dapol body on a kitbuilt underframe including parts from Parkside Dundas and ABS. Woodhead transfers and a degree of subtle weathering help to bring the model to life.

Parkside Dundas wagon kits have been around for many years now and are generally easy to assemble. Much of their range is invaluable for the early BR period modeller, whilst their 'Vanwide' kit, which appears in the illustration on page 4, portrays a prototype that lasted until the early 1980s.

to more than just a new coat of paint. The 1984/85 miners' strike substantially hit the Railfreight business and a resulting management exercise concluded that the way to improve economics was to make individual managers more responsible for their own spending. Wagons had already been allocated to pools largely based on commodity groups, and the allocation of locomotives to sub-Sectors on a similar basis emphasised the fact that assets and costs were under much closer scrutiny.

Early examples of locomotive pooling were for metals traffic from Teesside and petroleum products from Essex refineries. The locomotive naming policy at this time became a way of recognising the railway's major freight customers. One of these customers in particular, Foster Yeoman, having invested heavily in aggregate wagon stock, provided another harbinger of the shape of things to come in the acquisition of its own, American built, class 59 diesels introduced in 1986.

Soon each business unit was under pressure to make its sums add up. Many freight only lines supporting only one traffic could not bear their allocated infrastructure costs and closures followed. Despite the radical new imagery, all was far from well for Speedlink. It was constantly in danger of going the same way as the old wagonload order. The early discipline in train formations had been undermined by the drive to attract new traffic and the old bogey of 'tripping' costs was still rearing its head.

Speedlink had conveyed many of the lighter flows of traffic on a marginal cost basis but as the new accountability began to bite the bulk businesses chose to run their own trains more often. Even the engineers' departments set up their own 'Civilink' network, with dedicated wagon liveries. So the decline spiralled; Speedlink was left with only the poorest pickings, thus becoming even more uneconomic.

However, in fairness to the bean counters, it was hard to argue the case for a service in which the trunk haul

accounted for only 20% of costs whilst shunting and trip working swallowed up the remainder. The proposed 'Network 90' scheme echoed earlier plans in its attempts to trim costs, but it was too late to save Speedlink which was inevitably abandoned in July 1991.

Enter Enterprise Culture

Although Speedlink had ceased, some surviving traffic underwent a swing back to less frequent block working under the banner of 'Contract Services'. Notably, china clay formed the backbone both of these and of the short lived Tiger Freightways long distance freight services. Other examples include carbon dioxide for the Distillers plant at Cameron Bridge and timber from Scotland for papermaking.

In 1993, in the immediate run-up to privatisation, Trainload Freight and its assets was split into three operating companies, the assumption being that it might attract three separate buyers.

Initially these were known by their geographical territories but each company very quickly acquired a more imaginative name, which, of course, entailed more liveries! Loadhaul (previously Trainload North) adopted a striking orange and black whilst Mainline (Trainload South-East) had a distinctive bright blue with silver stripes. Transrail (Trainload West) more prudently settled for overbranding existing paintwork with its 'Big T' logo. The arrangement was not without character and some Mainline locomotives later emulated it.

But yet again wagonload freight was to rise from its own ashes. Transrail proved to be the most forward looking of the three companies and a major development was the September 1994 launch of its Enterprise network. This however is beyond the scope of this book, suffice to say that under privatisation and subsequent EWS ownership wagonload railfreight was still alive.

Modelling main line freight operations.

For modellers with enough space to build an extensive main line layout, browsing the pages of almost any general railway photographic album will reveal many varied freight train formations. However, for the vast majority of us with limited time and space at our disposal, we must find other ways of depicting our freight train formations. One way is to theme a layout towards the carriage of a particular traffic or commodity and research only the vehicles and loading facilities which are appropriate to the chosen period. This is an approach which we will return to in much greater depth in the next chapter, but to begin, we examine some possible ways of modelling main line freight.

The Block Vote
The 'block train, bulk traffic' culture is probably the main factor behind the oft voiced opinion that modern freight workings are almost impossible to model realistically. Whilst this view is justifiable in the larger scales, this may be the wrong way to look at the problem. Perhaps the type of railway scene we wish to depict should ideally suggest the choice of scale and gauge. Just as N gauge, or 2mm scale, is well suited to the portrayal of a railway in the landscape, as the Copenhagen Fields and Chee Tor layouts

exemplify, it is also suited to the modelling of long freight trains, not solely the prerogative of the British Rail era of course, but very much the popular image associated with trainloads of coal, steel, oil products and aggregates being moved between dedicated private sidings at each end of the journey

The term 'siding' in this context, although convenient, can be a misnomer, as facilities can include systems of enormous complexity servicing collieries, steelworks and the like. Loading facilities, too, for the more heavyweight traffics can be on the grand scale; some layouts such as Dave Peacey's original GCS Quarries have taken on the challenge of representing them.

For many years now, in both 2mm and 4mm scales, ready-to-run models and kits of numerous designs of wagon for the transport of bulk commodities have been readily available. In the larger scales too, kits have made a welcome appearance. So modelling trainload freight should, in theory, not be a problem. In reality, it is the space issue that is the difficulty, although some 2mm and 4mm scale layouts on the exhibition circuit have successfully depicted the trainload image complemented by similarly impressive main line passenger workings quite well.

A notable early example was the Bolton MRC's Darrowby back in the early 1980s. Recent ones include, in 2mm, Croyden Club's Acton Main Line, John and Steve Emerson's lamented Hayley Mills and Macclesfield club's Runswick Leamside. However, if space is tight, one solution might be to adopt the 'half sidings' approach as shown on page 50, which is equally suited to block trains.

The dominant image of trainload freight throughout our review period has been of high-powered diesel and electric locomotives trailing rakes of modern high-capacity wagons. Certainly layouts of the type just mentioned have reflected the image, almost always in the high profile sub-Sector period. However, both early and late BR periods highlight some apparently anachronistic but interesting combinations of motive power and wagon stock used on trainload freight that are worth considering for modelling.

BR had specified that air braking would be standard on all new wagon builds from 1966. The 100T bogie oil tankers of the time were exclusively so

Below. The original GCS Quarries layout, created in 00 gauge by Dave Peacey, portrayed rail borne aggregate operations in the late 1980s. Model locomotive types and wagons are readily available, though typically, representing this kind of activity in the larger scales requires a lot of space.

treated and consequently required diesel or electric haulage. However, the oil companies had been building up large fleets of modern four wheel tank cars with vacuum brakes since the late 1950s. These included the 35T type and some of the standard 45T type which are still around today. For the first few years of the British Rail era it was not unusual for block trains of these designs to be steam hauled (see page 10).

In contrast, by the latter half of the review period, the block working scenario was actually prolonging the life of dedicated rakes of traditional vacuum braked wagons despite the new type 5s being only air braked. For example, specialised steel coil and pipe carriers,

some converted from BCV and BEV bogie bolster types, were still quite youthful. Other residual vacuum braked block workings in the late 1980s involved flows of aggregates and industrial coal, whilst more unusual ones included sulphur from Mostyn Dock to Amlwch, and limestone from Wirksworth to Kings Lynn for sugar manufacture. Mostly these traffics used various mineral and hopper wagons of types MDV, MSV, HTV, HJV and HKV, (the classic 16t MCV having gone by this time). Perhaps the most interesting aspect of these combinations for the modeller was the contrast of the battered and rusted bodywork of the old wagons set against the locomotives in smart triple-grey livery.

However, before leaving the topic of block trains, it should be remembered that whilst converting and detailing ready-to-run wagons, or kitbuilding them in ones and twos may be enjoyable, the time involved in doing another twenty odd to the same standard for a block train will be very labour intensive and could well take the edge off your enthusiasm!

There is unfortunately no easy answer to this quandary, but there is often an intermediate level of detailing/finishing which can offer an acceptable compromise. Often just a little extra detailing and attention to minor livery variations can be enough to turn the better basic RTR vehicles into convincing models as the panel below discusses.

Upgrading and utilising bogie Iron Ore Tipplers

Since the early 1970s the blast furnaces of major UK steelworks had been fed with imported iron ores. Domestically produced ore was either all worked out or had become too expensive to extract. As a consequence,

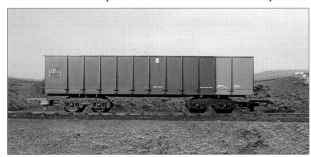

The Lima model as supplied. The livery is basically correct, obviating the need for a total repaint, but the bogies, being HO, are undersized. As supplied, the model is essentially a rake-end vehicle with a deeper headstock at the drawhook end (which should have buffers).

When modelling an inner vehicle, the bottom of the deeper headstock is trimmed off to match the one at the other end. New Cambrian bogies are assembled and fitted using suitable brass screws. Because the new bogies are of the correct scale size, new bogie centre holes and securing nuts must be provided 94mm apart. Finally add brake distributor and associated pipework fashioned from plastic rod and brass wire. Dummy

new train workings were introduced between certain ports and steelworks; namely Immingham and Scunthorpe, Redcar and Consett, Hunterston and Ravenscraig and Port Talbot and Llanwern. They were formed of the now familiar 100T air-braked bogie tippler vehicles of which the Lima 4mm example is a good basic model and an ideal candidate for upgrading. Moreover, they can look satisfyingly convincing in foreshortened block formations. The wagons have also been worked on limestone traffic into steelworks too. It would also be quite feasible to develop the theme and concoct a might-have-been steelworks somewhere in the UK to justify the vehicles in geographical locations other than the actual routes described above.

From inception the usual traction provided for these heavy trains was pairs of class 37s, although the South Wales run warranted a three loco lash-up until 1978 when they were replaced by pairs of 56s.

whitemetal Buckeye couplers are shown, but for fully working couplings on inner vehicles, fit Kadees or similar. The finished model, above, shows a rake-end vehicle, which must have correct drawing gear fitted (ie screw couplings and Oleo buffers). The model was fully repainted and is finished in a lightly weathered livery with a mixture of new lettering from the Woodhead, Cambrian and Fox ranges.

The Trunk Haul

Unlike the self-sufficient block loads described above, the trunk haul journey along a main line would usually see a variety of disparate vehicles and loads in one train. This was common to both the earlier traditional wagon services as well as the later air braked wagonload workings. In theory, such trains could include almost any type of wagon and arguably, offer more interesting modelling subjects. As with block loads, a larger, main line style layout, such as Aston Green (page 87) or Wallingford Road (page 93), is best suited to the portrayal of these trains.

In the late 1960s and early 1970s partially fitted class 7 freights were still common on most trunk routes. These consisted of vacuum fitted vehicles, often 12T vans, forming the front half of the train, with the bulk commodities, such as coal and steel, still conveyed at that time in unfitted vehicles at the rear. Some centres still sent out the old pattern of fully fitted express freight train in the evening, largely for the benefit of National Carriers traffic in traditional

vans and containers and devoid of brakevan. Again, any layout depicting a trunk route of the period could conceivably feature this type of train. One especially romantic working was the afternoon 'Scotch Goods' from King's Cross, often worked by a Haymarket class 40 with its consist including empty Blue Spot fish vans returning to Aberdeen.

Traffic losses and the contemporary introduction of TOPS were of course, instrumental in rationalising the diversity of types of traditional wagon thus care is needed when selecting freight vehicles for this period. The impact of TOPS was indeed total throughout BR train working, although one of its most obvious embodiments for the modeller was in the application of three-letter type codes to BR and many privately owned wagons.

By the time of the launch of Speedlink in 1977, the heaviest routes for the new air braked trunk trains tended to link the ferry ports at Harwich and Dover with the industrial areas of South Wales, the Midlands, the North West and central Scotland. Away from the central trunk, further flung destinations such as

Block freight trains on trunk routes were not always long ones. In 1988, 47 238 hauls just four chemical tank wagons on the daily service from the BP works at Saltend near Hull.

Inverness, East Anglia and Cornwall were catered for by short to medium distance feeder trains, and together with the trip workings considered later, there can be few areas of the UK which could not sustain a tenable Speedlink traffic in model form.

OWLs and GUSs

In the mid-1970s surviving traditional trunk freights on many routes shadowing the new Speedlink trains became

---

An approach to modelling long trains

Although some short block train workings did exist, most of the bulk commodity workings ran to typically twenty or more four-wheelers, or ten bogie vehicles of similar length to a passenger coach. Foreshortening of this on the model by reducing the number of wagons can diminish credibility. In similar vein, a long mixed freight presents the same space problem.

Is there an answer to this conundrum? Well yes, there is, but it all depends on your own choice of standards and the degree of compromise you are willing to accept. In general, the portrayal of bulk and trunk haul freights on main line routes require considerable space. For 4mm

scale, even with a sensible degree of compromise on train consist, a typical train would be some 10 feet long at least. Choosing N gauge is one way of reducing the area required but in 4mm or 7mm you have to be willing to accept greatly reduced train lengths. If that is so, then all well and good, and it is not for us to be critical of your choice.

Another solution for the space starved modeller follows on from the 'half station' approach, although in this context, it is the 'half marshalling yard approach', as shown in the accompanying drawing. Only the top end of a set of reception sidings are modelled, allowing the loco and the first few wagons to appear on

stage, the loco uncouples and proceeds to run round its train. To add additional interest, a passenger line could be included at the front of the layout running two car DMU services.

Such an approach would need only limited stock, but this would allow a high degree of detailing to be undertaken and would also be well suited to 7mm modellers too. We accept that this approach does not include the thrill of watching trains go by, as it is yet another convoluted variation on the atypical shunting layout, but as most railway modellers in the UK genuinely have precious little space we believe it to be a practical solution.

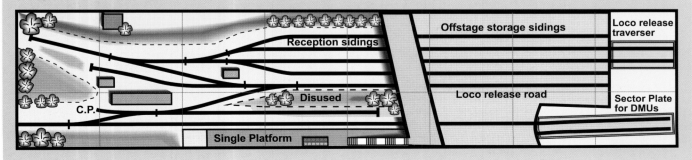

formally designated as the 'Other Wagonload' (OWL) network. However, as the range of traffic diminished, train formations became formed of maybe just two or three disparate 'mini-block' workings. Indeed by around 1980, the mainstays of these residual workings included MOD traffic in vans and opens, coal, steel, china clay, cement and grain.

The OWL train presents an interesting and under-exploited opportunity for running traditional freight stock at the height of the 'blue era'. It should be noted though, that the surviving vehicles were of what might be termed 'modern traditional' types, almost entirely BR standard design and vacuum braked, although unfitted coal wagons were initially fairly numerous. Earlier private owner stock like the

Distillers 'Blues' and tank cars for oil products have also been noted in such trains, along with the very occasional oddity like a gunpowder van.

Some quite heavy OWL trains linked several of the surviving big marshalling yards, including the Severn Tunnel Junction - Kingmoor services routed via the Settle and Carlisle line. Those from Toton to Acton, Eastleigh and Whitemoor were the last to convey heavy coal traffic in traditional vehicles.

By 1984 wagonload traffic was officially all transferred into the Speedlink network, but for another five years or so, there was a limited need for 'General Utility Services' (GUS), principally intended for conveying departmental materials and stores. In addition to well known civil engineers'

types such as the Dogfish and Grampus, these trains could include BREL stores vans and also the classic Esso 35T tank car, many of which were by then used for locomotive lubricating oil. A GUS could also include vehicles going for repair, parcels vans or air braked wagons, and conceivably the odd renegade revenue traffic falling short of an economic block load. One such recorded example is of Presflo cement hoppers. All in all the GUS principal is an even more anomalous and fascinating concept than the OWL, providing the opportunity to run varied but carefully chosen rakes of older wagons even in the sub-Sector period. We now turn our attention away from main line modelling scenarios and look at concepts that can be considered as being off the beaten track.

Freight off the beaten track.

The traditional blend of branch passenger and pick-up freight working has of course been the mainstay of hundreds, even thousands, of steam era layouts. A common misconception, which we are keen to dispel, is that the traditional pick-up freight and its associated wagons have no place on a layout representing the diesel or electric era. We have already lamented on the decline of the traditional pick-up during our review period but surprisingly, it did last in isolated pockets until the early 1980s.

Modelling rail freight operations off the beaten track encompasses all of the non-main line scenarios imaginable. This includes themes on trip freights, railhead terminals and freight only branches, all of which offer a wide range of possibilities for minimum space layouts.

The early part of our review period provides the best opportunities for the use of traditional stock, as depicted on Nigel Bowyer's well detailed and compact Carron Road and Elm Park 4mm terminii. Both these provide original angles on the combination of modern traction with pick-up style freight and plenty of operating potential.

The far flung corners of the network such as rural Wales and the Scottish Highlands also immortalised the traditional pick-up freight during this period and this latter area features in the panel on page 55.

The pick-up theme is also applicable to the yards of through stations on many UK secondary routes since, in reality, some such lines serving small market towns

did retain the last vestiges of these services through the 1970s. The most likely sources of revenue on these routes would be domestic coal, still carried in

Rural in nature, North Devon has given rise to a surprising amount of freight activity over the years. Our featured layout Lapford Road represents the line linking this area to Exeter and can operate a wide range of bona fide traffic alongside its passenger workings. In the period currently portrayed the transition from traditional freight stock is well advanced, a once weekly load of fertiliser for Lapford itself is worked as

an air braked company train, whilst daily carryings of milk and ball clay run in OWL format. Occasional traffics such as cement, steel plate and agricultural supplies are also included in this consist from time to time.

In this photo 31 101 runs into Lapford with just such a working. Empty ball clay wagons are bound for the line to Meeth. The 12t vans will be picked up from the siding.

Left. A typical Speedlink 'trip' working seen on the Cumbrian Coast line in the mid 1980s.
Below. Sheepwash portrays the concept of surviving freight only branches in the 1970s.

familiar vehicles like the 16T mineral and 21T hopper, and agricultural supplies such as fertiliser and animal feedstuffs in 12T vans.

So, despite the steadily declining use of such stock, British Railways-built standard vacuum braked wagons are entirely compatible with blue and even TOPS-numbered locomotives on this type of working. Occasional specialised wagons could still be seen in later years, one well documented example being gunpowder vans from an ICI explosives factory near Portmadoc on the Cambrian line. Also dependent on particular local requirements or occasional spot loads, other wagons in 'blue period' pick-ups might include a modern air braked van of BR, or privately owned, or even European origin.

Freight only branches and networks.
In the real post-Beecham world a common scenario was for a branch to survive as a railhead for just one or two major freight traffic sources, Redmire and Peak Forest being examples which at best were freight only 'branches' with just one commodity being transhipped. Others, whilst still branches in real terms, survived to carry more than one type of traffic. Two examples existed around the Torrington area in North Devon and must take some of the credit for the inspiration behind our featured Lapford Road and Sheepwash layouts. A few miles on from Torrington, Sheepwash depicts a scene in the final years of the meandering remnants of the former North Devon and Cornwall Junction Light Railway serving the ball clay works at Meeth and Marland. Until the end in 1982, the output of these works was carried in modest block trains of traditional short wheelbase Highfits and Clayhoods. In addition, agricultural produce in 12T vans was also moved as illustrated below.

Such rural freight only branches, devoid of any surviving passenger traffic and serviced by traditional stock, also survived well into the review period in numerous other places in the UK. Evocative 1970s prototypes with derelict stations and overgrown platforms include Horncastle and Louth in Lincolnshire, Blandford Forum in Dorset and Alloa and Forfar in Scotland. Freight only options as these, with an air of gentle neglect, are an unexpected slant on the branch terminus theme and offer challenging atmospheric modelling projects.

Although it is still relatively unusual for a British model railway to depict a freight only prototype, across the pond, such themes with credible provision of on-line industries and corresponding train formations are a cornerstone of much contemporary American railroad

modelling. Whilst we are not suggesting that we should all start modelling the railway scene in the States, perhaps a few leaves ought to be taken from their books.

All things considered, the more remote backwaters of our own rail freight system probably provide the nearest equivalent to the American 'short line'. The attendant trip workings being formed of a limited number of wagons serving a handful of industries. A British interpretation of the concept can offer ideal minimum space projects for both 4mm or 7mm scales.

We can loosely term these layout types as rail freight 'networks' and the branch to Flixborough, north of Scunthorpe, is perhaps one example of the theme. A layout plan based loosely on the idea is included in the panel below.

A number of other UK prototypes spring to mind also. Trafford Park in Manchester is a particularly relevant

example. It is a decidedly urban beast with ungated road crossings and lots of inlaid track and is remarkably similar to many an American style metropolitan industrial setting. Others in similar vein, though less urban, include dock systems, the Thornton Junction to Methil branch, the routes around Blyth, North Teesside and the Pyewipe area of Grimsby. These routes typify ones on which several railheads are strung out along the branch, some larger than others, some with block style working, some with wagonload working, some with both.

A layout on this sort of theme might reasonably be expected to occupy the walls of a room or attic with trip style working in the modern idiom. A well designed industrial setting might incorporate air braked Speedlink workings alongside OWL type services, with perhaps some engineer's traffic thrown in as well. Probably not cost

effective as far as the prototype is concerned, but as modellers, we do not need to be concerned about the economic viability of such activities.

The building of a new stretch of railway, whilst noteworthy today, has been on-going to a degree over the last 30 years. In the Mendips stone quarrying area a limited amount new railway construction was involved at three quarries. However, a more ambitious example of latter day freight railway construction is provided by the scenic clifftop line from Boulby mine in North Yorkshire. In 1974, several miles of the old Middlesbrough to Whitby line were reopened south from Skinningrove to move potash and salt from the mine. The link required a deviation from the old alignment and the construction of a new concrete viaduct.

Given a strong enough traffic base, such as with mining or quarrying, and

---

A freight only wharf layout

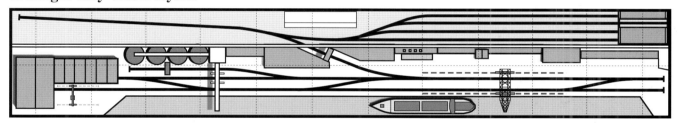

Above. An overall view of Flixborough Wharf. The huge cranes would require considerable scaling down on a model.

Right. Steel traffic heads to the wharf. 08s mainly operate on the branch.

Making molehills out of mountains is one way of describing the process of adapting the prototype for a modelling project. This layout combines the features of New Holland and Flixborough freight terminals which are both riverside wharves.

The salient features from each site are included; grain silos, warehousing and wharfside with scaled down gantry cranes. To keep the off stage sidings within the overall dimensions they are accessed via a hidden kick-back head shunt. Trains are made up in the sidings and propelled by the locomotive back into the head shunt. They then run forward through the scenic break

and onto the layout proper. Considerable compression of the original sites has taken place but even then, quite lengthy trains can still be operated.

As envisaged the layout would be operated in the air-braked era with steel wagons, vans and Polybulk hoppers making up the mainstay traffic. Equally, spot loads could also be catered for which could include coal containers, chemical tankers, and oil vehicles. In fact, almost any commodity that can be transferred to or from a ship into rail vehicles is feasible.

Left. Ian Manderson's 4mm Easington Lane layout is set in the mid 1970s. It incorporates two railheads serviced by traditional wagonload freight in the classic mould. A sparse DMU passenger service provides additional interest on this well designed minimum space scheme.

sufficient environmental benefit, the Boulby example shows that the idea of actually reopening a redundant line could believably be applied to many other parts of the country for layout purposes. The principle could extend to coal, nuclear waste, MOD traffic or docks traffic.

Freight Railheads and Terminals

These sites provide boundless opportunities for small layout ideas. Ian Manderson's Easington Lane is one particular example which combines two speciality railheads and a truncated passenger branch in a very economical space of 8ft x 2ft 6ins. It depicts the mid 1970s when the effects of Section 8 grants had yet to make a significant mark.

Obviously motive power had undergone a radical change over the preceding decade, but as hinted on page 52, in some areas there had been an interlude when it was almost business as usual for traditional wagonload and sundries traffic. As briefly mentioned earlier, from around 1968, some goods sheds and yards, like those at Scarborough (Gallows Close), Bangor and St Austell were operated by National Carriers for sundries carryings. Indeed at Truro, a new goods warehouse with private siding connection was installed as late as 1972.

Other former goods yards developed into specialised use; a group of nine steel handling terminals being a noteworthy mid-1960s development in the Black Country. The term 'Public Delivery Siding' gained currency for locations with minimal facilities which were often no more than an old siding with a hardstanding for transhipment to or from road vehicles. Such a 'yard' was used by just one or two specific customers rather than for a whole range of commodities. A plain loading bank requires little in the way of maintenance and even when overgrown can be brought back into short term use for spot traffic.

Returning to the topic of Section 8 grants, many freight movements required heavy investment to allow transfer to rail. In an increasingly road orientated market, Section 8 was intended to tip the economic balance in favour of rail and a primary criterion was the environmental benefit that would be realised by cutting down on lorry movements, especially in rural areas.

Investment covered by the grants could include land purchase, track and earthworks, buildings, loading bays and facilities and even fork lift trucks.

In 1986, at around the peak of Speedlink, there were some 800 terminals available to handle wagonload traffic and nearly as many again serving trainloads. This was admittedly a fraction of the figure thirty years earlier, but does show the potential for modellers of the period allowing the invention or adaptation of traffics and terminals to suit their own preferences.

Below. P. D. Stirling's depot at Mossend, Glasgow is an example of a modern style urban railhead.

With Section 8 grants, the railhead concept might be thought of as being synonymous with long trains, big air braked wagons and all the trappings of modern handling facilities and operating practices. Certainly categories of aggregates and industrial minerals often benefited and such traffic receives further consideration in the next chapter. However, we have previously touched on the notion of how a little modellers' licence can provide slightly more imaginative interpretations of reality in the best traditions of railway modelling. Thus even small terminals served by short cuts of wagons can be concocted with credibility allowing authentic portrayal in compact layout format.

Whatever the chosen period, and whether they form a layout in themselves or are part of a larger one, modern freight handling facilities provide almost endless opportunities for fine detailing and cameos incorporating small buildings, loading sheds and gantries, road vehicles, fork lifts and all the general detritus of any working environment. There are many such detailing items available from the manufacturers, but a point perhaps worth mentioning is that pallets, nowadays common enough to be classed almost as litter, were not general in distribution work until the mid-1970s.

Urban Railheads

It is not difficult to include urban rail freight terminals in the 'off the beaten track' category as they provide a further source of original and absorbing prototype material worth modelling.

Earlier we mentioned the rundown of the traditional station goods yard and the continued survival of some under the control of National Carriers. The larger cities had possessed more dispersed freight facilities, some of which were also vested in NCL. Many commodious Victorian goods warehouses shambled into the 1970s with the same air of fitful slumber and forboding as some of the grandiose city passenger stations we mentioned in chapter 2. As the years progressed, the one time lengthy rakes of Vanfits and Conflats that could be spotted at these localities were typically succeeded by parcels stock or even a desultory few air braked vans of the new generation before final closure ensued.

For the modeller with a sideline interest in high Victorian architecture,

Scottish branch freight traffic

Scotland provided many interesting secondary routes running freight in the traditional mould. The Highland routes to Kyle of Lochalsh, Wick and Thurso, all featured very much the classic passenger/ freight mix in the mid-1970s and inspired our featured layout 'Kyle of Tongue'. Together with the odd steel mineral for domestic coal, staple agricultural traffic was mainly conveyed in BR standard 12T vans. Domestic electrical goods for a high street retail chain were also transported in standard vans to Thurso until the early 1980s. Refrigerators and washing machines being off-loaded into the archetypal white Luton van parked up on the hardstanding would certainly make an unusual cameo.

Various types of specialised wagon can easily be justified alongside traditional stock on a '70s Scottish theme layout. As illustrated here on 'Kyle of Tongue' a small fuel depot and a supposed off-stage distillery were both served by early examples of the resurgent private owner wagon. Parcels traffic is also in evidence with a CCT and a GUV in the train consist.

Heavyweight freight traffics for Highland theme layouts include trains of large diameter pipes and cement products for construction traffic associated with North Sea oil and gas extraction. Such services ran to depots at Strome Ferry and Invergordon. Sadly, by the dawn of the Sprinter era, freight north of Inverness became very sporadic.

On the other hand, freight workings on the West Highland routes to Oban and Fort William came to prominence with much resurgence in the Speedlink era. Despite this latter day renown, however, the lines could earlier boast quite a selection of freight traffics encompassing the inherent change from traditional to specialisation - oil terminals, timber, paper products, finished aluminium and the ingoing raw material, alumina, together with fish and general goods for ferry quays serving the outlying islands.

As an alternative to the well frequented Highland theme, the secondary lines of Buchan in North East Scotland

offer an interesting contrast. Whilst the long branches to Peterhead and Fraserburgh lost their passenger services in 1965, freight lingered on to eventually cease in 1979. In earlier times these routes had interestingly been a haunt of the North British type 2.

All the above provide interesting traffics and wagon types for various timescales on a model Scottish outpost. The real advantage of the railways in this geographical location is that shorter freight (and passenger) trains were generally the norm and the whole package lends itself well to adoption by space starved modellers, even in 0 gauge.

such depots would make an absorbing project and provide an atmospheric centrepiece to a layout. Due to their size the larger structures would perhaps be ideally suited to a 2mm scale setting, although the Leamington club's Walford Town nicely depicted one in 4mm scale that was conceived to be still in use in the 1980s.

In the Speedlink growth period of the 1980s there were many instances of distribution firms with existing road fleets opening their own rail served depots. These involve modern steel portal frame buildings with both road and rail access and are readily adaptable for layouts with urban settings. The Glasgow area had several private terminals serving the immediate hinterland, including Deanside Transit, Isis-Link and P.D. Stirling. Between them these handled a very wide range of commodities, including animal feeds, Campbell's soup, baked beans, soft drinks, imported fruit and bonded goods. Such van traffics require little in the way of specialised unloading facilities. Another high profile case was the Stockton Haulage depot at Stranraer, set up initially for steel exports to Ireland via the Larne ferry, but which was also used for other traffic.

Spot Loads.

Although Section 8 investment required a degree of permanence and stability, other promising opportunities for the modeller are provided by more transient traffic flows, the so-called 'spot' loads which are of short term duration but nevertheless, profitable.

Transhipment facilities for spot traffics are often basic or improvised, such as with the examples pictured overleaf. They can very easily be superimposed on an existing layout to add a little variety to an operating session. They can occur for the carriage of a surprising number of products. Certainly agricultural traffics adapt well to the concept; fertiliser and grain being a prime example, but equally, other such commodities as finished steel, pipelines, raw timber and molasses have all been seen in such circumstances.

In recent years EWS have trialled freight workings to many places from which it has long been absent. These have included Kyle of Lochalsh, where one of the quay sidings was relaid, and fertiliser to Great Yarmouth, unloaded at little used carriage sidings. Even preserved railways have generated freight traffic, the best known probably being the Fitzgerald Lighting traffic in VGA vans from the private siding at Bodmin. Such recent initiatives can easily be backdated into

Continental spot loadings

In 1984 this German Cargowaggon vehicle was photographed in a goods siding at Malton in Yorkshire. Although the true reason for its visit was never established, speculation suggested that the firm of Bright Steels Ltd., in nearby Norton, could have used it on spot import or export traffic. Certainly a concept that can easily be included on any layout configuration, large or small.

Although models of similar style vans have been available in HO for some time, we have included a drawing in 4mm for modellers who may wish to create a fine scale version. Construction could be achieved mainly in plasticard, although brass plate for the main underframe is recommended for rigidity. All the door and roof ribbing could be created using Microstrip. The German plate bogies have been available as a 4mm kit from Appelby Model Engineering. Livery is silver with a blue band and white Cargowaggon lettering. The VTG logo is in black.

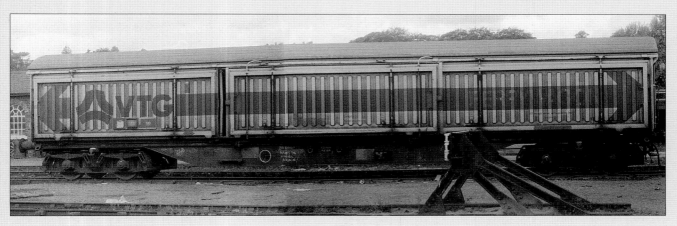

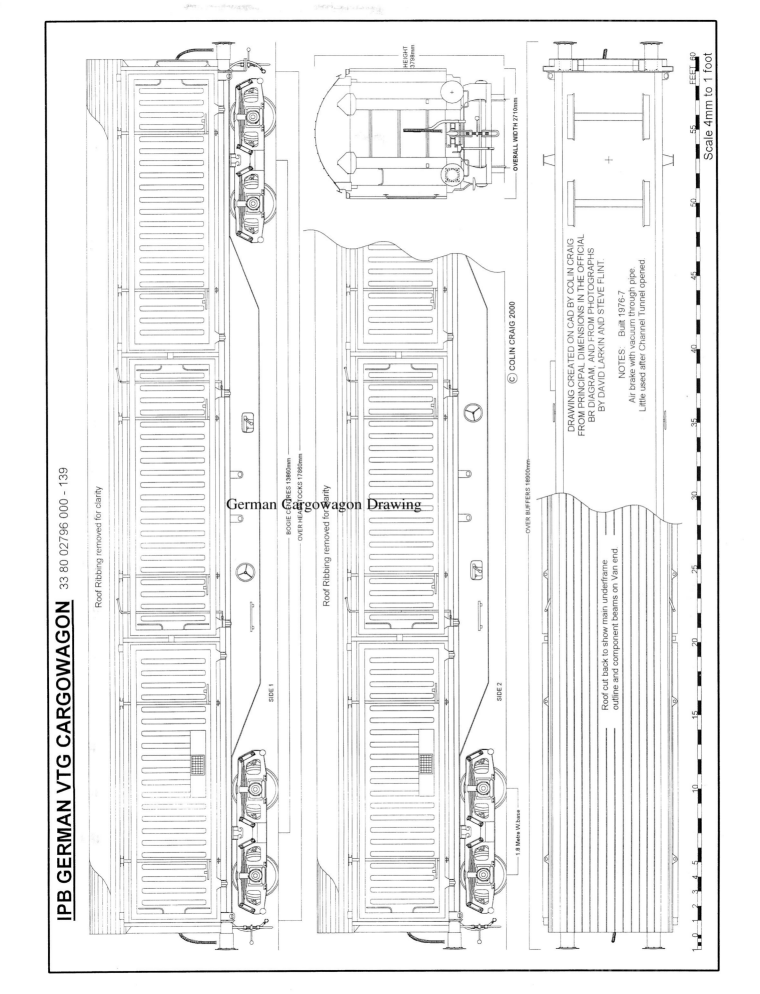

IPB GERMAN VTG CARGOWAGON 33 80 02796 000 - 139

German Cargowagon Drawing

Roof Ribbing removed for clarity

Roof Ribbing removed for clarity

SIDE 1

SIDE 2

1.8 Metre W/base

BOGIE CENTRES 13860mm

OVER HEADSTOCKS 17660mm

OVER BUFFERS 18900mm

© COLIN CRAIG 2000

HEIGHT 3798mm

OVERALL WIDTH 2710mm

Roof cut back to show main underframe
outline and component beams on Van end

DRAWING CREATED ON CAD BY COLIN CRAIG
FROM PRINCIPAL DIMENSIONS IN THE OFFICIAL
BR DIAGRAM, AND FROM PHOTOGRAPHS
BY DAVID LARKIN AND STEVE FLINT.

NOTES: Built 1976-7
Air brake with vacuum through pipe.
Little used after Channel Tunnel opened.

Scale 4mm to 1 foot

FEET 60
55
50
45
40
35
30
25
20
15
10
5

Above. This probable spot load traffic in traditional 12t vans was seen at Beverley in 1977. Unloading was straight into road vehicles parked on the hardstanding, the nearby goods shed was not in use at this time.

Right. Fertiliser in huge polypropylene sacks was a short term loading on the Far North line seen here in OAA opens at Lairg in 1986.

the Speedlink era to provide the additional interest which would be missing with a more literal replication.

Stock exchange

The vast marshalling yards of the Modernisation Plan are hardly practical prospects for layouts even in the smallest modelling scale, Z! However, smaller banks of exchange sidings are modellable in their own right, as indeed we briefly touched on in the panel entitled; An approach to modelling long trains. By developing the principle a little further, such siding facilities can be presumed to serve harbours or dockyards, chemical works, industrial process plants large or small, power stations and the like.

Moreover, neither the facilities nor their associated rail systems need to be modelled at all. Indeed the whole plant need only appear as a distant hazy embodiment on the backscene with the layout itself just featuring a few yard roads, a run round loop and some modest railway buildings. Colnebridge, one of our layout themes on page 91, is a similar scheme, it assumes that the sidings serve a large industrial chemical plant just conveniently offstage on the left.

Such typical schemes can provide considerable shunting potential and countless hours of fine detail modelling on the chosen wagon types. There are many traffic sources which can provide a basis for this approach and most can be easily adapted to the years within our review period.

On the topic of shunting, diesel types had been a very early introduction into

this work and by mid-1966, the time honoured 0-6-0 tank locomotive was down to double figures in BR stock. The multiplicity of diesel shunter designs was also thinned out and the 350/400hp class 08 and its derivatives came to be the widespread standard by around 1970. Notable exceptions to this were the well known uses of classes 03 and 06, and an authentic setting for one of the other smaller types could furnish the basis of a late 1960s shunting layout.

A private network can, of course, provide justification for a company owned industrial shunter built from one the many enticing kits currently available from specialist manufacturers. Like their BR counterparts they make attractive models. However, it should be borne in mind that the number of industrial locomotives dropped dramatically from

the 1960s due to the same reasons as the BR shunting fleet. A tenable application should really have both sufficient traffic on offer as well as a suggestion of an extensive enough track layout offstage. Exchange sidings, trip workings and the smaller terminal facilities underpin a lot of modelling opportunities from the BR era and serve to link the foregoing historical comment with the next chapter. This goes on to study in greater detail a number of key freight traffics which we believe have a particular appeal for the BR period modeller.

Included under each topic is a detailed consideration of the wagon types used and a review of the associated loading and unloading facilities.

Below. Speedlink is the cornerstone of freight activity on Reighton and features spot loadings of bagged malt interspersed with regular trips of grain.

Chapter Five

Freight Modelling Focus

The selection of freight flows under closer examination in this chapter have been chosen on the basis that they are representative of the BR era and offer lots of potential for the modeller.

The latter point is somewhat subjective, of course, and to some degree the choice has also been influenced by those freight flows that we have a particular affinity for.

That said, however, we hope that the subjects will open up some fascinating opportunities for further study in both these and the multitude other topics that we have been unable to cover. The aim is to help modellers tune into the very spirit of BR railfreight activities.

Any one of the following studies can either be used as the basis for a small self contained layout, to which many of us are restricted anyway, or altenatively, provide a number of add-on traffic sources for a larger layout.

Domestic coal in the British Rail era

This basic commodity was responsible for the origin of Britain's railways and continued to account for about half of BR's freight revenue during our review period. Modern coal traffic will inevitably be symbolised by the omnipresent pit to power station Merry-go-round operations, but, as impressive as these workings are, there have been many other facets to coal transhipment by rail.

In this brief insight into this huge subject, we look into some latter day domestic coal operations. This traffic has traditionally been an easy prospect for modellers and very few model goods yards could be considered complete without a small coal staithe providing standage for the archetypal 16 ton steel mineral wagon or the pre-nationalisation wooden private owner. Unloading was always manual - by men with shovels.

The North Eastern Railway pioneered the use of hopper wagons for domestic coal and often the smallest of station yards were equipped with suitable drops, where, in British Railways days, the LNER-inspired 21T hopper wagons reigned almost supreme.

With the closure of many local yards, the philosophy of coal concentration depots emerged which were intended to be served by block trains of 21T hoppers. These mechanised railheads covered much larger areas, with onward distribution by road reducing the need for trip freights.

However, such large depots were not as widespread as might be thought. There was certainly more centralisation, but

Domestic coal wagons in the '70s & '80s

As the post war replacement for the small privately owned coal wagons of earlier years, those 16 ton steel minerals still running by the 1970s were a sufficiently important resource to warrant major bodywork repairs. This included anything from patchwork replating up to full body replacement and rebuilding. The classic Airfix kit and the more recent Bachmann model are probably the definitive 4mm scale versions.

Examples are shown here in the typically weathered forms in which they were so often found amongst the surviving domestic coal yards of the 1960s and 1970s. Some of the more distinctive patterns of corrosion were often as a direct consequence of early repairwork.

Over the years hopper discharge assumed greater prevalence on this traffic; the HBA/HEA (below) air braked types took over the carriage of domestic coal into the Speedlink era and beyond. Versions of these hoppers are readily available in the major scales as either ready to run or as kits.

When originally introduced as the HBA version in 1976 they appeared Freight Brown livery, which some still carry to this day. The Flame Red and Grey Speedlink livery first appeared on the last few wagons built in 1979, although the red aspect quickly weathered to a dull tone of soft pink!

some smaller depots handled moderate numbers of the 21T vehicles and many surviving coal yards in the old style continued to receive 16 tonners. Upgraded facilities replaced the old labour-intensive unloading methods and included grab buckets mounted on conventional road cranes and hydraulic rams to raise one end of a wagon and tip the load through the end door.

Overall, domestic use of coal has obviously declined over the years, but in the mid-1980s sufficient tonnage remained to justify an attempt at transferral on to the Speedlink network. Likewise aimed at the centralised depots, some local yards without hopper discharge facilities had been brought up to date by the development of economical portable conveyors. Others, like at Gobowen, were simple undertrack discharge pits adjacent to the station.

There had always been more resistance to centralised railhead distribution from the Scottish merchants, and with less use of the main alternative fuel, natural gas, this market was one with greatest potential growth. Thus in the interests of flexibility the Scottish operation incorporated an amount of inter-modal working using privately owned containers on BR-owned wagon chassis. These wagons, designated FPA, provide an interesting alternative to MGR style trains and a 4mm drawing is included in the panel opposite.

In recent times, there has been an increasing trend towards loading and unloading wagons by grab, particularly with short term spot flows, and modern flat bottomed mineral wagons have thus been built as a simple basic box without side doors. The MEA conversions of the HEA hopper, first seen in 1990, have been produced by Bachmann on the HEA chassis, and privately owned designs have included Tiger Rail's POAs on redundant 45T tanker underframes.

There has also been increased use of purpose built containers on various miscellaneous flows.

Right. The FPA coal container can be easily modelled in 4mm by using the standard Hornby 20ft 9ins underframe (as fitted to SAA and VDA models). The containers could be scratchbuilt in plasticard on a batch basis. Although predominantly a block train working, shorter cuts of these wagons ran in Speedlink trains as illustrated on page 45.

Right. 25 036 stands in Burnley coal depot in 1982. Coal is discharged into an undertrack bunker and raised by conveyor for storage.

Below. A similar set up, still in use, exists at Gobowen where the undertrack bunker is immediately adjacent to the passenger platform and canopy.

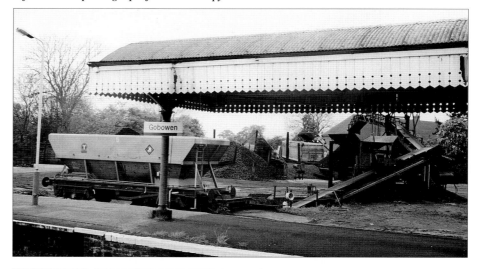

FPA COAL CONTAINER WAGON

400XXX

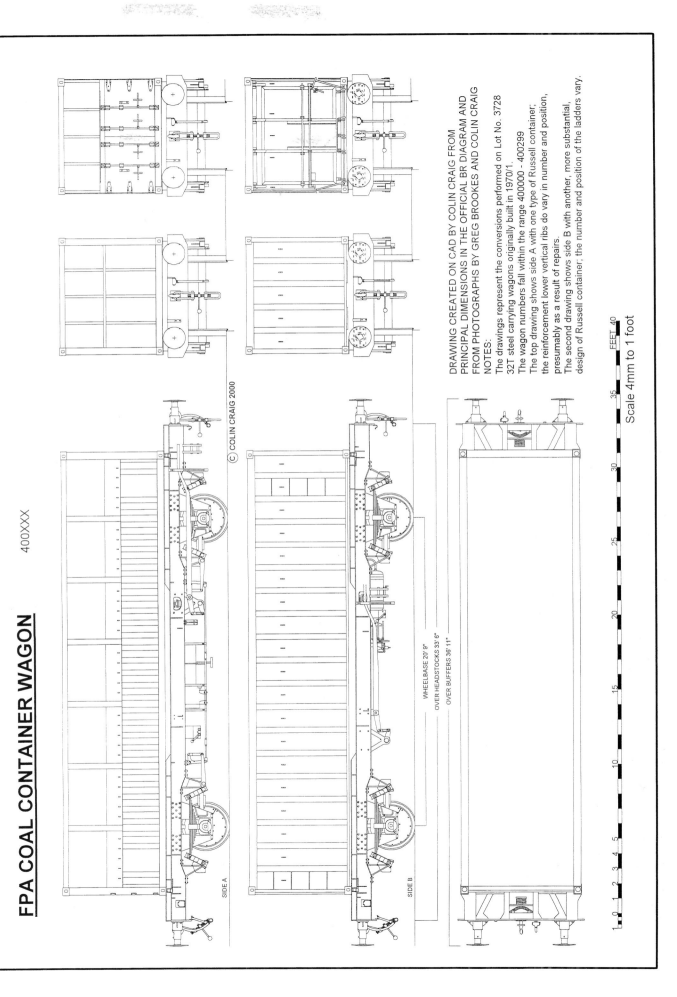

© COLIN CRAIG 2000

SIDE A

SIDE B

WHEELBASE 20' 9"
OVER HEADSTOCKS 33' 6"
OVER BUFFERS 36' 11"

DRAWING CREATED ON CAD BY COLIN CRAIG FROM
PRINCIPAL DIMENSIONS IN THE OFFICIAL BR DIAGRAM AND
FROM PHOTOGRAPHS BY GREG BROOKES AND COLIN CRAIG
NOTES:
The drawings represent the conversions performed on Lot No. 3728
32T steel carrying wagons originally built in 1970/1.
The wagon numbers fall within the range 400000 - 400299
The top drawing shows side A with one type of Russell container;
the reinforcement lower vertical ribs do vary in number and position,
presumably as a result of repairs.
The second drawing shows side B with another, more substantial,
design of Russell container; the number and position of the ladders vary.

Scale 4mm to 1 foot

A Cut with the Grain

Another commodity that has long been popular with modellers is grain traffic. Whether this is because of the colourful wagon types that have been associated with it, or down to its vital role in the manufacture of certain popular drinks, no one knows for sure!

A major development which brought grain wagons to the notice of contemporary modellers was the large fleet of custom built hoppers owned by wagon leasing firm BRT. These were introduced from late 1965 to transport barley for Scotch Whisky production and were hired by the Distillers group for their traffic between East Anglia and various Scottish destinations.

With their bright blue colour scheme and large advertisement boards for Distillers brands, these vehicles considerably raised the profile of the humble grain wagon from that of the small and less distinctive types which had originated with the pre-Nationalisation companies. There was also a smaller fleet introduced for Associated British Maltsters which carried a yellow livery, but despite this, the wagons became colloquially known as the 'Blues'.

The Distillers and ABM operations were essentially block train flows. They

were based on a number of loading points in the Eastern Counties and along the East Coast Main Line corridor, the locations of which varied over the years. Wagons were tripped in small cuts through East Anglia to Whitemoor Yard and eventually combined into a trunk haul formation at Doncaster. This in many ways presaged later Speedlink patterns of operation. Upon arrival in Scotland, most block trains were split up and tripped out to numerous destinations with suitable unloading facilities.

This Anglo-Scottish grain traffic continued through the late 60s and early 70s but dropped off prior to the 1980s, meaning that both Distillers and ABM wagons were under-utilised and thus available for use on grain flows in other parts of Britain.

However, the grain sector was still seen as a lucrative market and, in an attempt to win back traffic, the 'Grainflow' initiative was launched in 1980. This was a partnership between BR's Railfreight sector and wagon hirer TSL, who already had experience of Polybulk wagon operations on the Continent. The objective was to bring grain traffic under the umbrella of Speedlink operations using air braked

Above. Grain traffic on Reighton depicts the Anglo-Scottish flows in 1983 when air braked Polybulks were just replacing the BRT hoppers.

wagons. A batch of Polybulk vehicles were acquired and appeared in the tasteful and now familiar green and grey 'Grainflow' livery.

Grainflow's subsequent success in revitalising the railborne grain market was bolstered by a further batch of dedicated Polybulks in 1983 and also encouraged Distillers to investment in a fleet of new Polybulks themselves. These also appeared in 1983 to a slightly different design and received a striking pale grey and blue livery. They replaced the ageing fleet of Distillers/BRT blues, some of which continued in service for a few more years on other industrial traffic.

The diverse loading and unloading points for Anglo-Scottish grain operations can provide endless opportunities for layouts set in eastern England or north east Scotland. Our featured layout Reighton portrays just such an operation set in 1983 in rural East Yorkshire at the time when the new Distillers Polybulks were just being commissioned.

Whilst the Distillers business is perhaps the most celebrated of grain

Grain wagons and the British Rail modeller

The BRT blue liveried hoppers (above) appeared on ECML Anglo-Scottish flows in the mid 1960s. Many were refurbished in the 1970s, receiving pedestal suspension. A revolution in general grain carriage came with arrival of the high-capacity air braked Polybulk hoppers. First seen in the mid-1970s, these imposing vehicles have since been irretrievably associated with Speedlink and EWS grain flows. No commercial model of a Polybulk has yet appeared in 4mm scale, and this is surely a missed opportunity in view of the great variety of liveries and the range of traffic applications to which they can be put. Perhaps the several distinct designs of these wagons complicate the issue; conversions are possible from Continental sources, although the inevitable scale difference from 3.5mm scale does have a bearing. The Electrotren model is a good starting point for conversion to the Scottish Malt Distillers Polybulk (opposite) and can convey the impressive length quite convincingly. For 2mm modellers, the N Gauge Society produces a straightforward kit of the more common 'Grainflow' Polybulk (right).

Traditional types too have been a little under appreciated, the old Hornby Dublo model of the BR standard 20T design (illustrated right) being unfortunately well short of scale length. K's old whitemetal kit for the GWR Grano is a rarity nowadays, although the Parkside kit for the characterful LNER wooden van is easily found.

In being basically a dedicated covered hopper, all generations of grain wagons have from time to time also found employment on other powder traffics. Notable 'blue period' examples have been redundant Blues and Minibulks on alumina traffic from Blyth. There are others which are worthy of research for the modeller who likes the wagons but perhaps wants a more unusual angle on their usage.

The Blues have been the subject of models in 4mm scale from several manufacturers and in 2mm scale, Peco have marketed versions for many years. A batch of Blues was refurbished and converted to air braking in 1983, becoming part of the Grainflow fleet (as depicted by Lima's rendition of the 'Minibulk').

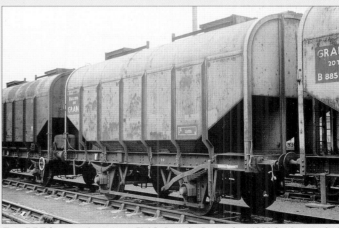

Top. BRT hoppers in store at Keith Jnct. in September 1983 having worked their final grain loadings. An interesting variation on weathering is evident on this example.

Centre. A pair of Grainflow liveried Polybulks on the grain railhead at Kennett in East Anglia in May 1988. Subtle variations in livery can be seen.

Bottom. The traditional BR standard 20T grain hopper could still be seen on certain UK brewery traffic well into the early 1980s.

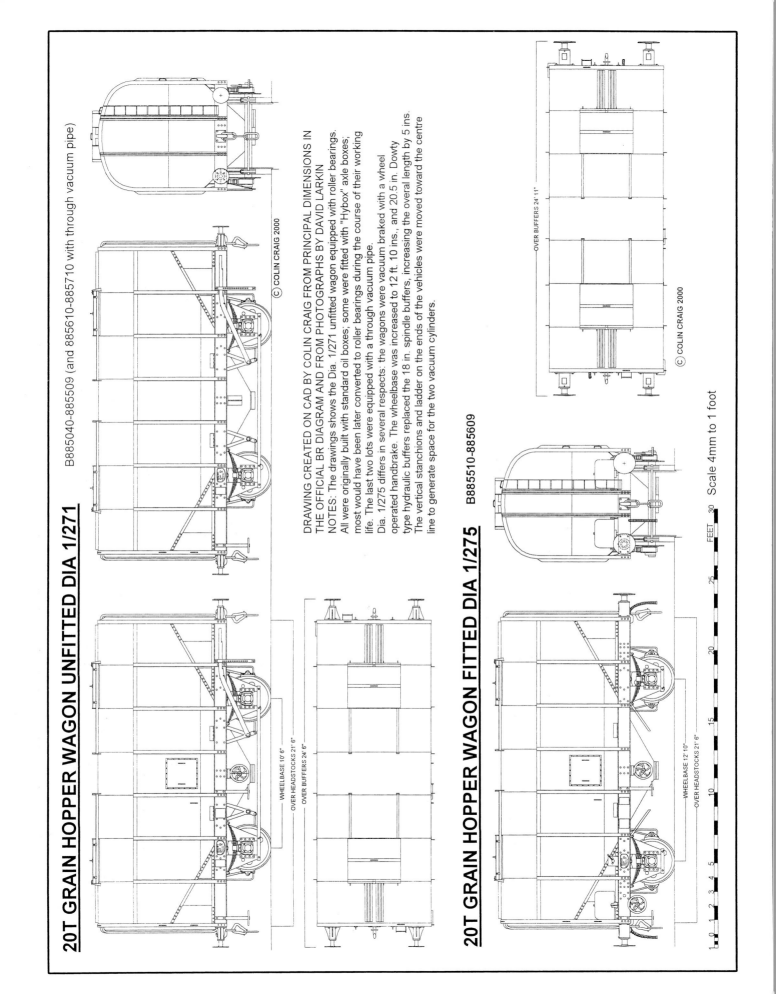

20T GRAIN HOPPER WAGON UNFITTED DIA 1/271

B885040-885509 (and 885610-885710 with through vacuum pipe)

WHEELBASE 10' 6"
OVER HEADSTOCKS 21' 6"
OVER BUFFERS 24' 6"

© COLIN CRAIG 2000

DRAWING CREATED ON CAD BY COLIN CRAIG FROM PRINCIPAL DIMENSIONS IN THE OFFICIAL BR DIAGRAM AND FROM PHOTOGRAPHS BY DAVID LARKIN

NOTES: The drawings shows the Dia. 1/271 unfitted wagon equipped with roller bearings. All were originally built with standard oil boxes; some were fitted with "Hybox" axle boxes; most would have been later converted to roller bearings during the course of their working life. The last two lots were equipped with a through vacuum pipe.

Dia. 1/275 differs in several respects: the wagons were vacuum braked with a wheel operated handbrake. The wheelbase was increased to 12 ft. 10 ins., and 20.5 in. Dowty type hydraulic buffers replaced the 18 in. spindle buffers, increasing the overal length by 5 ins. The vertical stanchions and ladder on the ends of the vehicles were moved toward the centre line to generate space for the two vacuum cylinders.

OVER BUFFERS 24' 11"

© COLIN CRAIG 2000

20T GRAIN HOPPER WAGON FITTED DIA 1/275

B885510-885609

WHEELBASE 12' 10"
OVER HEADSTOCKS 21' 6"

FEET   Scale 4mm to 1 foot

0 1 2 3 4 5   10   15   20   25   30

Grain handling facilities.

Above. Newmarket terminal. Although the main storage and handling facilities were of much more modern construction, some older maltings architecture is evident here at the rear of the depot.

Left. The grain reception terminal at Dufftown in North East Scotland saw use throughout the 1960s and 1970s, but stood gaunt, disused and trackless in this photograph taken in 1995.

Above. A similar structure for unloading bulk grain was located at Muir of Ord on the Far North line out of Inverness. Twin covered discharge bays are seen on the right. Lorries would be loaded beneath the storage silos for onward distribution by road.

Immediately after harvest, grain must be dried to prevent it from decay during storage, typically this requires the water content to be reduced from around 40% to less than 10%. Grain dryers can often be located on farms themselves, but for bulk handling larger facilities involving vertical oil or gas fired drying kilns are used. Once the grain is dried it is transferred to storage in the familiar cylindrical silos to await either further processing or transhipment.

Rail wagons are top loaded by fixed augers and conveyors which are generally suspended above the track on a gantry, as reproduced on Reighton, or simply

cantilevered out at high level from the adjacent building.

At the destination point, the contents of the hoppers are discharged into a pit between the rails and the grain is once again raised mechanically into a silo for eventual transfer into lorries, such as at Muir of Ord and Dufftown.

In modelling such structures some selective compression in height is sensible, alternatively representing the buildings in low relief is an option.

Many such facilities, of course, pre-date Speedlink and Grainflow practices, although the Norwich Division of British Rail was expert at pushing the benefits of

Section 8 grants and such classic installations of the Speedlink years could be found in East Anglia. One such loading facility, at Eccles Road between Norwich and Ely, was actually over half a mile from the main line and is thus a prototype example where only the exchange sidings need to be modelled.

The depot recently featured in the much reported revival of grain traffic by EWS and in both instances Polybulks were moved over the connection by an adapted JCB tractor; a novel possibility for the adventurous modeller, although a more conventional industrial or ex-BR shunter would be just as plausible.

workings, the wide variety in other rail borne grain traffic must not be overlooked. The import and export of grain and related products provided more revenue for Speedlink as a result of Britain's inclusion in the EEC agricultural policies of the 1980s. This was most evident at east coast ports, like

Kings Lynn, Ipswich and Tilbury, with traffic originating from the nearby production areas and also other localities the UK with a suitable arable output.

Facilities processing grain and its derivatives, for instance, flour and animal feed mills, are also often located in dock areas, some notable examples being

Birkenhead and Leith. Ports exporting grain conveyed by Speedlink have included Barry, Sharpness, Avonmouth and Southampton.

Lesser known examples of similar traffic in the '80s included the orange liveried STS Polybulks, built for a short lived import operation of grain and

Grain handling facilities (cont).

A grain loading point on a layout need not be as space consuming as that depicted on Reighton. If the adjacent dryers and silos are assumed to be offscene, then just the loading gantry and elevator need be constructed. The structure featured on Reighton is based on the prototype at Kennett and illustrated below. The drawing is to 2mm/ft scale.

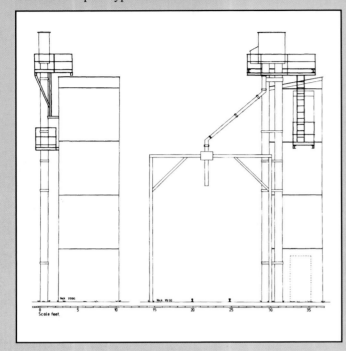

cereals through New Holland, and the similar Tiphook vehicles of the late '80s.

Thus, all in all, the portrayal of grain traffic has many facets and not all require huge or complex facilities. At the opposite end of the scale, spot loading at improvised road/rail terminals, with just a mechanical auger for transhipment, is equally feasible and authentic.

Grain traffic was a major casualty of the abandonment of the Speedlink network in 1991, but, as the foregoing has illustrated, there was a decade or so of interesting air braked workings to inspire the modeller.

Polybulks and Blues apart, traditional designs of grain hopper still operated well into our review period, being accommodated within less obvious scenarios well away from the East Coast strongholds. In the 1960s and early 1970s the surviving GWR, LMS and LNER built vehicles were all worked as a common pool with the BR standard variants (see panels on pages 63/64) and can thus be used with authenticity on a layout representing any region.

One promising example is the traffic that originated on the Wallingford branch

in Oxfordshire, notable since Western Region locomotive classes are perhaps less obvious in conjunction with grain hoppers (see page 93).

Another use for barley, of course, is in brewing. The famous brewery at Burton on Trent, and the lesser known Alloa Brewery in Fife, were still being served by traditional railway-owned hoppers well into the late 1970s. From the modelling perspective it is therefore not inconceivable that, in the early British Rail era, a small independent brewery could be located in many a market town and receive such wagons in just ones and twos.

Locomotive types on Anglo-Scottish grain traffic

For over twenty five years the classic grain trips of East Anglia featured haulage by the ER stalwarts of classes 31 and 37. Once combined at Doncaster, the class 40s were mainly associated with the trunk haul north, although other type 4s often did service on this part of the run and 37s were noted too. At the Scottish end, with terminals at Muir of Ord, Burghead, Dufftown and Leith, haulage by the Sulzer type 2 variants or, later, Highland 37s can usually be justified on a layout.

Distillers wagon trips in the York area, to and from the exchange sidings with the celebrated Derwent Valley Light Railway, were provided from time to time

with less usual traction combinations. This ranged from York depot allocated class 20s in the late 1960s and early 1970s to a borrowed LMR 25/2 recorded in 1978. Another unusual use of class 20s with the Blues was on the surviving remnants of the Speyside branch in the 1960s shortly after their introduction.

Earths and Stones

Under this general heading we have included a variety of heavy mineral traffics which comprise almost anything mined or quarried other than coal. The topic is again huge and comprehensive coverage would require a separate tome in itself. Thus for our part, and taking heed of our comments in the previous chapter, we have selected a few choice examples that we hope are of appeal to the average modeller.

For the main part of our review period the predominant traffic has been aggregates; mainly sand, gravel and crushed rock. However, a diverse range of industrial minerals formed nearly half of the erstwhile BR 'earths and stones' category. Some of these are perhaps better suited to smaller layout themes.

Firstly however, aggregates, whose growth in consumption was well timed for the resurgence of bulk rail freight. The increased demand was due to a construction boom fuelled by massive road development and investment in public and private buildings, which, especially in the South East, was outstripping local resources. Block trains of sand from Essex pits had worked to the Capital since the 1960s but the Mendip quarries in Somerset provided the now legendary aggregates operations.

Most of us will undoubtedly associate aggregate workings with the new generation of Type 5 locomotives and modern air braked high capacity wagons. However, in many cases, traditional wagons were used to establish new aggregate flows before the air braked wagon designs appeared. Thus shorter rakes of vacuum braked tipplers and hoppers could be seen at many localities on sporadic spot aggregate trains, even into the late 1980s.

Most quarry loading installations do tend to be on the large side, especially those incorporating the crushing plant, as depicted on GCS Quarries and latterly

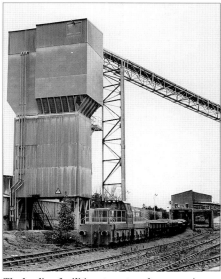

The loading facilities at most modern quarries are huge affairs and when modelling, some selective compression is necessary. This loading tower at Tilcon's Swinden quarry near Skipton, is however quite stylish in comparison to some. A smaller facility can be glimpsed to the rear.

Modelling modern industrial railway buildings

Common to many industrial structures after the 1960s is the construction method. Brick and concrete almost universally gave way to steel portal frames covered with cladding, such as corrugated asbestos and GRP sheet. Doors and windows also became minimal. For the modeller this is a distinct advantage, construction is much simpler and quicker and there is a huge range of moulded, embossed and milled plastic sheets available. Wills and Slaters sheets are familiar, but a greater variety is produced by the American firms Pikestuff and Evergreen.

Construction requires a simple structural shell in Plasticard or thin ply to which the cladding is secured using contact adhesive. With smaller buildings, a shell may not be necessary.

The key to success is with the painting and finishing. Use matt paint and weather so that the recesses in the sheet appear slightly darker, adding fine white dry-brushing to create highlights on the raised corrugations.

Milled sheets were used to construct the stone hopper on Ian Saunders' Cranleigh Down (above). Wills box cladding, Slaters brick sheet and Peco window and door frames make up the industrial unit on Reighton (right).

The Redmire loading chute

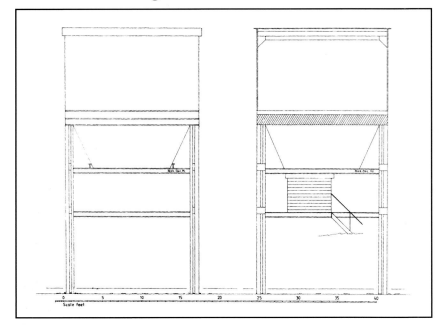

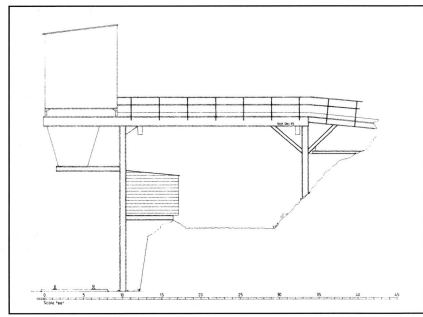

by its new owner on RM Quarries. However, at the customer's end, unloading can be carried out in a simple covered bunker with conveyor system. Short and medium term traffic flows can be catered for by a length of hardstanding and a grab-equipped tractor.

An alternative approach involves the frequently documented loading facility on the Redmire branch which was used for crushed limestone associated with Teesside steel foundries. Its very compactness makes it particularly interesting to modellers and such a structure could be readily adapted for aggregate loading. A detailed study appears in the accompanying panels.

The Redmire example brings us nicely round to industrial minerals traffic. In contrast to the foregoing, this kind of traffic occurred in shorter block flows and which, under Sectorisation, was operated by different divisions. Principal here is iron ore and the imported variety was covered briefly on page 49.

UK extracted iron ore declined in the 1970s but sufficient sites hung on to provide an interesting traffic source for modellers. The Eastwell Group's unique modular layout depicted just such an example - part of an Oxfordshire ironstone works and its associated exchange sidings set during the 1970s.

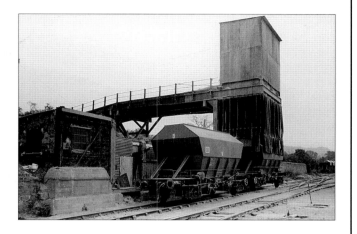

The Redmire loading chute is a rather ramshackle looking structure but served its purpose well. Tipper trucks loaded with crushed rock reversed over the ramp and tipped their load into the chute which in-turn discharged into an empty hopper wagon below. The chute accommodated one wagon at a time, each being manually shunted by gravity. The drawings (opposite) are reproduced at 2mm/ft scale. A model would be very easy to build, again with Plastruct and plastic embossed sheets, the polythene dust sheets (hard to replicate) could be left off.

Although used by air braked block trains which were split up on arrival and reassembled on departure, the chute is easily adaptable to any quarry location and particularly for those modelling the earlier flows with vacuum or unfitted stock in short rakes. Thus a rail borne aggregate themed layout in a small space is entirely feasible even in 7mm scale.

Although the layout was large and ran a huge variety of stock, its principal traffic featured short rakes of diesel hauled ore tipplers. A theme that can be replicated at many other localities in the UK, such as Cumbria or Northamptonshire. Other industrial minerals transhipped by rail include salt, lime, sand, gypsum, soda ash and alumina. Many of these substances have properties akin to dry powders and can be pressure loaded or discharged like cement, thus Covhop, Presflo, Prestwin and Cemflow vehicle types can be used.

Alumina is well known for the trains from Blyth terminal to British Alcan plants. A local working to the plant at Lynemouth was one of the last unfitted revenue service trains to run in the country, although the Covhop wagons used were not quite what they seemed. They were actually built in 1971 as updated versions of the original design. Alumina traffic in Scotland made use of

Below. The British Alcan terminal at Blyth in 1986.

The alumina loading facilities at Blyth.

There are two loading towers at Blyth of different height, the lower of the pair probably being the optimum size for a suitable model.

Construction would be simplicity itself, being nothing more than a box of corrugated sheeting. Some glazing is evident here and there. Storage silos would of course be assumed to be offstage unless modelled in 2mm.

the BR owned Presflos and for a short time in the '80s, as a stop-gap measure, some of the by then redundant BRT grain hoppers were drafted into service on the Fort William run along with PAB covered hopper wagons (see drawing opposite.)

The Alumina loading facilities at Blyth consists of a pair of relatively simple covered hoppers that will be easy to model. Essentially they are little more than GRP clad vertical towers and are illustrated above. The huge bulk storage silos would probably benefit from being off scene!

Soda Ash was a good earner for BR, certainly in the area around the ICI works at Northwich. In the '60s and '70s, the most common wagon for moving this was the standard Covhop. However, ICI also used a version of the TTA tanker (as per the Hornby model) for these workings and even found use for some 16t minerals

on short flows in the North West. These were hired 'private' examples which had aspired to sheet rails, a jolly good clean and ICI livery. They were only a stop-gap and were phased out during the late

1970s when air braked modern tank wagons were drafted onto such services.

PAB Covered hopper No. PR8005 (BRB 1255) seen at Mossend Yard in October 1988. This shows a vehicle fitted with leaf spring suspension.

PAB COVERED HOPPER WAGON PA005B PR8001-8049

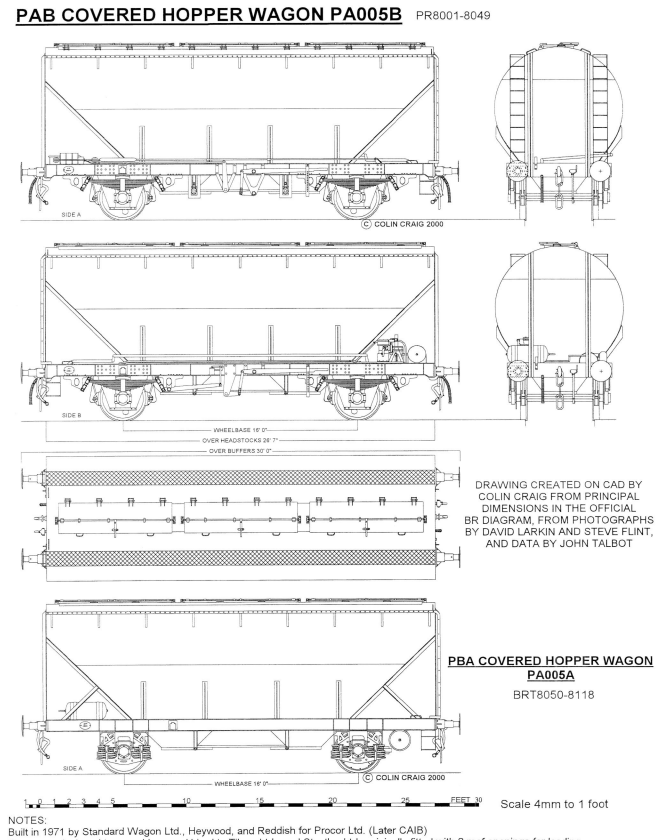

SIDE A

© COLIN CRAIG 2000

SIDE B

WHEELBASE 16' 0"
OVER HEADSTOCKS 26' 7"
OVER BUFFERS 30' 0"

DRAWING CREATED ON CAD BY
COLIN CRAIG FROM PRINCIPAL
DIMENSIONS IN THE OFFICIAL
BR DIAGRAM, FROM PHOTOGRAPHS
BY DAVID LARKIN AND STEVE FLINT,
AND DATA BY JOHN TALBOT

PBA COVERED HOPPER WAGON PA005A

BRT8050-8118

SIDE A

WHEELBASE 16' 0"

© COLIN CRAIG 2000

Scale 4mm to 1 foot

NOTES:
Built in 1971 by Standard Wagon Ltd., Heywood, and Reddish for Procor Ltd. (Later CAIB)
They were designed to carry Lime, and hired to Tilcon Ltd., and Steetley Ltd., originally fitted with 3 roof openings for loading
and two bottom discharge chutes. Some were hired to Alcan Ltd. for movement of Alumina, and some of the wagons used
for this traffic were subsequently modified to have 4 circular loading hatches. These can be identified in photographs;
examples of this modification were PR8004, 8005, 8024, 8035, and 8036.
They were airbraked from new, but were also fitted with a through vacuum pipe.
The design was very similar to PBA design code PB005A, BRT8050 - 8118, also shown above, built by Standard Wagon for BRT
in 1972/3, and leased to BSC; the major differences were the use of ESC Friction Pedestal suspension with disc brakes, wheel
operated handbrake, and the absence of a through vacuum pipe.

PRA CHINA CLAY WAGON RLS6303 - 6316

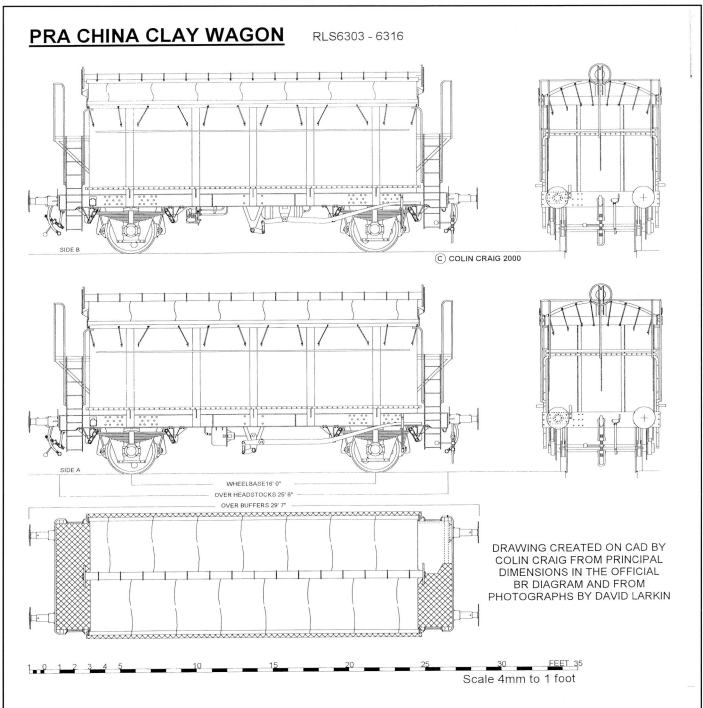

SIDE B

© COLIN CRAIG 2000

SIDE A

WHEELBASE 16' 0"
OVER HEADSTOCKS 25' 6"
OVER BUFFERS 29' 7"

DRAWING CREATED ON CAD BY
COLIN CRAIG FROM PRINCIPAL
DIMENSIONS IN THE OFFICIAL
BR DIAGRAM AND FROM
PHOTOGRAPHS BY DAVID LARKIN

0 1 2 3 4 5 10 15 20 25 30 FEET 35

Scale 4mm to 1 foot

NOTES:

Built in 1983 by Standard Wagon Ltd., Heywood and Reddish for Railease Ltd., using chassis from redundant APCM pallet vans originally built in 1964 to Dia. 6/492.

They were designed to carry China Clay, hired to Wiggins Teape Ltd., and used between Cornwall and Corpach, near Fort William. The underframes were fitted with air brakes during the conversion which allowed use on Speedlink services.

They had a relatively short working life, with the last few remaining vehicles being stored out of use by 1992; this was probably due to a change to hopper discharge wagons and/or slurry tankers offering more efficient handling for this type of material.

PRA No. RLS6306 at Tiverton Junction in March 1983. The end platforms and tarpaulin hoods make these vehicles particularly distinctive and interesting.

Feat of Clay

Whilst on the topic of 'powder' commodities we thought this old favourite was worthy of inclusion too. Although documented heavily in the contemporary railway modelling press during the preparation of this book, we still felt the subject warranted further coverage. We do hope that you share our sentiments?

China clay traffic from Cornwall has long been surrounded by an enchanting air of romance and nostalgia. A captivating appeal that is perhaps as much to do with the wagon types and working practices as to the area from which it originates.

Conjuring a mental picture provides an image across which Clayhoods rattle by, probably at Golant in deepest Cornwall, hauled by a class 37, 46, or 50. This combination of large diesels, old fashioned wagons and pleasing scenery is undoubtedly an attractive prospect for modelling, but, dare we say it, this isn't the whole picture. There is much more to replicating this traffic in model form than at first meets the eye and, to trap the unwary, some strange myths have arisen over the years.

One myth is that all clay traffic is powdered china clay (kaolin), a high grade kaolinite compound, often referred to as 'White Gold'. Certainly, its most common form for shipment, particularly for export, is in the powder state (1%-2% moisture), although the product can be supplied in pellet form (10% moisture) and in liquid slurry form (20% plus). Increasing amounts in liquid slurry form began to be moved by rail from the mid 1960s. The main use for china clay has long been in connection with paper manufacture where it used as a bulking and glazing agent.

However clay traffic also encompasses the movement of a lower grade kaolinite compound known as 'Ball Clay' which is more glutinous in makeup and extracted using mechanical excavators. Ball clay production occurs in Devon and Dorset and is more usually sold on in 'shredded' (ball) form although it can also be transhipped as a powder, a slurry, or as pellets called 'noodles'.

Above. Empty Clay Hoods and clay opens rattle through Lapford Road behind a 31 on route to Sheepwash on the line to Meeth in Devon. As far as is known the hoods remained in the South West throughout their lives.

Below. China Clay sites are full of atmospheric little hideaways crying out to be modelled. Here, an articulated Cargowaggon skulks at the back end of Trevalour clay dries in October 1988.

Both types of clay are still used extensively in the ceramics industry for numerous applications and have many other lesser, though no less useful applications in such things as; chemicals, fertilisers, insecticides, leather making, paint making, pharmaceuticals, rubber and plastics.

At the start of our chosen review period, clay of both types was still carried in sheeted open tippler wagons. These were the purpose built 5 plank 'claytip' vehicles from the 1950s. Built to Diagram 1/051 on 9ft wheelbase underframes, they were basically updated versions of the style of wagon introduced by the GWR at the start of the 20th century. All the tipplers were finally

vacuum braked by the early 1970s (the first 300 out of the 875 built were originally unfitted). 12T standard vans were used to move smaller consignments which were shipped in bagged form.

China clay traffic patterns within Cornwall involved numerous workings from pits to local harbours where the product was transhipped into waiting vessels. The WR's class 22s played a leading role in these activities from their introduction in 1959 until final withdrawal in January 1972. Shorter trip workings provided employment for a small number of 08s. Services were worked in time honoured fashion much as they had done over the previous 70 years or so. The traditional scene had

been one of small, busy engines and hordes of small, clay stained wagons shunting amidst the surreal lunar landscapes of the clay pits or trundling down luxuriant valleys on their way to oft picturesque little harbours.

However, by the mid '60s operations were about to start changing. Around this time, BR was looking to extend the principle of block train working, though as far as the internal (Cornwall) china clay traffic was concerned, they'd already been doing it for years!

On traffic that went northwards to Stoke and Scotland, and eastwards to Kent, this had not been the case. Thus, in 1965 the 'Clayliner' service was introduced, though in no way did the wooden bodied opens used in the block formations on these runs really match up to their rather pretentious contemporary title. A jumble of 10ft wheelbase ex-company 5 plank opens, together with some BR standard ones, were drafted in to make up the rakes of sheeted wagons. As a concession to modernity, the majority of the stock used on these services were fitted with roller bearings, the long distances involved being justification for the expense. Also the ex-company stock included in these fleets at the time were also upgraded with BR 'W' irons. These minor modifications provide the modeller with an opportunity to include a little variety on the otherwise standard five plank wagons of the Clayliner fleet.

These small improvements however were soon outpaced by further progress. At around the time of the introduction of the above services, English China Clays (ECC), the major producer of china clay, and paper manufacturers Bowaters, were looking into the possibility of moving the clay by rail in liquid state as slurry.

This led to the 'Clayfreighter' service to Kent, though this time, state of the art, air braked tank wagons were employed

Above. 25 216 winds past Golant on the branch to Fowey. This picturesque scene is in stark contrast to the lunar like landscapes associated with clay pits and drying sheds. Both scenes however creating a unique and interesting modelling mix.

Right. Wagons used on Clayliner services offer challenging prospects for weathering as E 262820 clearly illustrates. Replacement planks scrounged from unserviceable stock contribute to the wagon's shabby appearance, especially when the original lettering is still in place.

(a model, crude by today's standards, was once produced by Triang Hornby). This service provided one of the first regular turns for class 47s on clay traffic as they were the only WR locomotives available at the time capable of working the air braked tanks.

The success of the Sittingbourne traffic demonstrated that moving china clay as slurry was ideally suited to the paper making process. Having made this first quantum leap, progress continued albeit slowly and by the late 1960s slurry tanks also began running to the Scottish paper makers.

Meanwhile, the Clayliner fleet carried on through the 1970s with only minimal visual changes, though due to age, and the ravages of the commodity carried, they became increasingly piebald through both the number of replacement planks needed, and the onward march of rust. One modification that was used for both fleets was the fitting of zinc sheeting on the floors of wagons where decay was causing contamination to the product.

The Clayliner turns gained some notoriety during the early to mid '70s for providing regular freight work for Westerns, at least as far as Bescot. This class of loco being used on these trains

almost up to end of their existence on BR (Reputedly, this was to stop the LMR "borrowing" WR allocated class 25s!).

Away from all the tinkering with the old 'tubs', real strides were being made with further wagon developments commencing in the mid 1970s. Air braked stock became much more common on the longer haul services, often as a result of ECC's success in gaining new customers. For example, bogie Cargowaggon vans and the high capacity Polybulks made their way across the channel for both bagged and bulk clay bound for the Continent. These improvements were not just restricted to overseas traffics as privately owned covered hoppers and bogie slurry tanks began serving Scotland and the North West respectively.

BR even got in on the act by using their various types of air braked van on UK bagged traffic. Gradually the mix of wagons became ever greater and thus increased the variety and potential for modelling this traffic along the way.

It was also at about this time that the ubiquitous Clayhoods made their entrance. The spur for this being the projected development work at the Port of Fowey. The pitched tarpaulin hoods

were the result of several experiments to provide a 'user friendly' way of covering the cargo to combat water contamination. It must be said that they were basically no more than a stop-gap, since ECC and BR both knew that the wagons were out of date, but no one was able to find the capital to replace them. Thus, in 1974, the familiar blue hoods appeared on 674 of the tipplers. Some of these were branded, rather subtly, for Ball Clay use, by the addition of a thin horizontal yellow stripe at the bottom of the hood. This conversion scheme was not applied to all the available wagons of this type and some unmodified vehicles survived into the early 1980s running as part of the Clayliner fleet.

Evidence suggests that the Clayhoods were used only on the internal Devon and Cornwall traffic. It is possible that some of the 'hoods' flew the nest from time to time, however, as we haven't yet unearthed any photographic proof so far, the jury must remain out on this matter.

In 4mm, models of the Clayhood are currently available from Bachmann and, as a kit, from Ratio. These examples are models of prototypes fitted with roller bearings and, as such, are rather uncharacteristic of the Clayhood fleet.

Locomotive types on china clay

Immediately following dieselisation, the West of England clay traffic was mainly powered by NBL type 2s (22s), with 350hp shunters (08s) on local workings. Whilst Swindon's Warships saw service on this trade, by 1962 they'd graduated onto higher things. However, most interestingly in our period, Warships on clay were again to be seen until 1967 in the shape of the NBL D600 series (41s).

The Clayfreighter services introduced the class 47 to clay duties during the mid 1960s. Not a type readily associated with these workings, but their influence slowly increased to the point that, by the early 1990s, they had a large share of the traffic on offer. Back to the early 1970s, Sulzer powered traction appeared in the form of class 25 and class 46. The 25s began to appear from 1971 and were intended as direct replacements for the 22s, which by the beginning of 1972 were phased out in line with the National Traction Plan. The 25s put in much good work, though by the time of their departure in August

1980, they had mostly gravitated to Devon area workings. The 46s, drafted to the WR from 1969 onwards, were mostly used on the heavier workings. Despite eradication of the 46s in 1984, the BR/Sulzer type 4 outline survived a couple of years longer in the shape of their LMR allocated class 45 brothers, seemingly 'borrowed' from their allotted NE/SW passenger turns.

What of the Westerns?. With their abilities in demand elsewhere on the region, they never reached a point of ascendancy on clay traffic. That said, they did see regular use on the many of the longer turns, as mentioned in the text. Those that had gained air brakes were even used on the Clayfreighter tanks when the more usual class 47 was not available.

The ubiquitous class 37s first saw use on china clay work during 1978, taking over from the class 25 turns.

True to form, they proved to be masters of their tasks. Such was their acceptance that during 1983, they became the only class to receive the short lived 'Cornish Railways' markings. (Cornish

Railways plus flags on the nose, the double arrow on the body in red with an entwined lizard). The class fulfilled their role on clay traffic well beyond the BR era, though by the time of writing, their days look numbered. The late 1970s saw the first use of class 50s on some services however, their presence was more prevalent during the 'large logo' era. A high point for the class was the allocation of the sole Railfreight class 50, 50149, to St Blazey in 1987.

Finally, we'd also mention the use in Devon of class 31s, the class being in sole charge on the Meeth line in its last year as indeed portrayed on Sheepwash.

China clay loading facilities

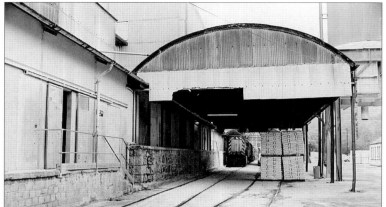

Left. The works and dries at Ponts Mill in 1984 with 08 945 shunting PRA wagons. The loading dock and quaint canopy could be modelled against the dries buildings constructed in half relief to save space.

Lower left. The same scene taken from the back end of the works showing another canopy. The compactness of scene oozes atmosphere and is perfect for modelling in a small space. Interestingly, there was no run round loop at Ponts Mill so all trains to the works were propelled along the branch, the ex-Southern Railway brake van being used as a 'propelling brake van' to assist the operation. Sadly this little gem was demolished following the end of train services in 1992.

Below. Another shot of the Trevalour works with 50 045 'Achilles' nosing nonchalantly through the site. In-laid track is a common feature of such places. Note also the subtle difference between original asbestos cladding, on the left, and the new GRP cladding on the building to the right.

A layout based on a clay handling facility need not be set anywhere near the clay pits themselves. More often the hydraulically mined clay (slurry) was piped from several pits to a centrally located drying point. This is in itself useful for modellers as the spoil tips from mining are big, in fact very big!

The clay 'dries' were busy looking sites where rail facilities often went right into the heart of the plant. By our review period, the surviving sites had been modernised with new refining plant, settlement tanks and gas fired dryers. This upgrading often left the old 'dries' buildings redundant and derelict, although sometimes they were re-used, for example, as at Moorswater, where they formed part of the warehousing used to store rail borne cargo.

In general, buildings at clay drying sites are large affairs and in the most unsuitable for true scale modelling in any scale. Half relief drying sheds combined with loading platforms and canopies would be a practical compromise. A particularly memorable layout which used this approach was Ian Metcalf's 'Pengwynn Crossing'.

The loading of wagons with the bulk product during this time was, and still is, mostly carried out by front loading mechanical shovels. The sidings being inset into a concrete apron to aid the operation and also to allow for loading of road vehicles from the same warehouses. This method of loading can be applied whether the waiting wagon is a Clayhood, a 13t open from the Clayliner circuit or an air braked Clay Tiger hopper. Some bulk loading is carried out in covered accommodation.

Bagged and palletised clay loads would be fork lifted into awaiting vans whilst a simple overhead gantry frame and loading pipe would be used for the filling of slurry tankers.

Smaller loading facilities, well suited to the modeller were to be found at Teigngrace in Devon. Here, they consisted of a high concrete platform some distance from the dries which was served by a looped siding most of which was inset in concrete.

The reception points at the traffic destinations are usually much smaller prototypes. The new clay railhead at Stoke on Trent, for instance, is nothing more than a short, open-ended GRP cladded shed positioned directly over the unloading pit.

Finally, of course, if you are just interested in modelling stock, the reception/exchange sidings approach is entirely feasible with the clay workings again a distant feature on the backscene.

Above. A delightful and seemingly anachronistic mix of rolling stock types is evident in this shot of Parkandillack taken in June 1987 with 'Red Stripe' Railfreight liveried 37 675 as centrepiece.

Although roller bearings were virtually universal on the Clayliner 10ft wheelbase highfits, the belief that roller bearings were fitted to all the Clayhood vehicles is another myth. In actual fact, only a few Clayhoods appear to have been so fitted, this being done in the mid 1980s, post-dating the demise of the Clayliner services. Those so fitted were most likely done as a matter of expediency, using up available spares from ex-Clayliner opens. Observation suggests that the vast majority of 'hoods' carried plain boxes to the bitter end.

Returning to the longer distance traffic, by the early 1980s it had become increasingly apparent that the fleet used on the Clayliner runs would not hold out much longer. Customers still wanted the product in powder form, so, for replacement stock suitable air braked wagons were sourced from the private sector. In 1982, with the aid of a section 8 grant, a new terminal at Cliffe Vale, Stoke on Trent was opened and new air braked bogie hoppers, the 'Clay Tigers', were brought into service. Of course, the modern vehicles had many advantages over the old 13 tonners, their greater carrying capacity meant fewer vehicles were needed and their air brakes and higher permitted speed allowed the traffic to be conveniently absorbed into the Speedlink network.

Sadly though, the need to update wagons spelt the end for the line to Petrockstowe in 1982. To accommodate the new vehicles, the track would have needed renewal and with the amount of traffic on offer, it could not be justified. So, the Clayliner trains with their rakes of sheeted wagons passed into the history books. The Dorset railhead facility at Furzebrook, on the truncated Swanage branch, did survive into the air braked era due to better track condition.

The years following these events saw an ever increasing variety of air braked stock. The 'jewel in the crown' probably being the use of Polybulks to Switzerland which commenced in 1976. Other wagons being of particular note were the Standard Wagon PRA box wagons, and, notable for their use on the UK's longest freight run from Burngullow to Irvine, were the large 'depressed centre' slurry tanks, better known by their nickname of 'Silver Bullets'.

Returning to internal Cornish clay traffic, by the mid '80s the problems associated with the age of the Clayhoods became ever greater, and after much prevaricating, during which time the traffic could have transferred to road, BR took it upon itself to provide replacements for the veteran wagon fleet.

Initial trials with a specially cleaned HAA in 1986 proved successful and from this evolved the hooded CDA derivative of this design. 115 of these were built new to this design at Doncaster works during 1987 and a further 24 were added by converting surplus HAAs from the MGR fleet. Like the Clayhoods they replaced, the CDAs' lives seem to revolve solely around the West Country internal routes.

In February 1988, the Clayhoods ran in anger for the last time, ending over 70 years of traditional working. After many years of change, those from 1988 to 1994 saw relatively little.

As mentioned in the introduction, this subject is quite involved and this overview can only, at best strive to be a 'thumbnail sketch' of BR's dealings with clay. For those of you wishing to know more about this traffic, publications which go into the subject are included in the bibliography.

Oil and Chemical Traffic

Rail tank traffic enjoyed a boom period from the 1960s conveying a wide variety of fluid and gaseous commodities. Oil and associated derivatives had been railborne in bulk tankers for some years but now substances ranging from powerful acids, liquefied gases and hydrocarbon solvents became commonplace. Such tank traffic can be readily adapted to almost any BR model railway layout, both in block train format and as short rakes of wagons in trip freight mode. Certainly during the Speedlink era, short chemical or oil trips were a common sight up and down the length and breadth of the country.

Tank Wagon Developments.
Petroleum and associated chemical products have been carried by rail from the 1870s. Tonnage steadily rose in the

Oil Terminals

The larger oil terminals, such as those at Thame and Leeds East, illustrated on page 80, require considerable areas of baseboard, even in 4mm. Thus, smaller facilities, such as at Fort William and Lairg (right), are worth considering for modelling if a more compact design is sought. Although set in Scotland the design is basically universal and can be readily adapted to many other rural localities in the UK.

Certainly such depots seem to consist of generally standardised facilities and security fitments, presumably to conform to fire and safety regulations. Normally one or two sidings can be seen surrounded by a chain link fence with the exit protected by a set of steel gates. Discharge pipes located between the sidings and several bulk storage tanks, both of vertical and horizontal design, are fairly usual.

In contrast to Lairg, the terminal at Greetland in West Yorkshire (lower right) is an example of a slightly larger facility serving a more urban hinterland. The canopy over the road tanker loading area also appears to be a common feature to such sites (see Thame photo).

Knightwing's pipework kit could be put to good use here for the discharge piping and oil storage tanks could be quickly scratchbuilt from household plastic waste or drain pipe. However, for speed and ease of construction, the Ratio oil depot kit is ideal. Two have been used to good effect on Nigel Bowyer's Elm Park layout (right).

Below. A detail view of the discharge pipework at Greetland depot. The Knightwing kits are ideal for replicating this feature in 2mm, 4mm and 7mm scales.

20th century as the UK began to consume more and more oil. New tank designs were developed to handle this booming traffic. The first major development came in 1957 with the 35t tank developed between British Railways, Esso and Charles Roberts and made legendary by the Airfix/Dapol 4mm kit.

This was soon followed with the 'Monobloc' design which incorporated a larger diameter tank barrel positioned in between the solebars. Tankers to this new design began entering service from 1960. The now familiar bogie oil tankers of 102t glw, began to appear in traffic from around 1967 following successful testing of prototype vehicles built a year earlier.

Meanwhile, advances in tank wagon design also benefited the movement of chemicals. Liquid Petroleum Gas (LPG) tank wagons appeared in 1963 and received a livery of white for the tank with a horizontal orange stripe at waist height distinguishing them from other petroleum wagons. Tank barrel sizes varied according to the density and volatility of the load. An interesting example is the 46t liquid chlorine tank built by Charles Roberts in 1967/8 A model could be readily scratchbuilt in 4mm scale using a standard 15ft Hornby underframe, although at the time of writing, reports suggest that a new version of the underframe may soon be available from Bachmann.

The 1980s saw ownership of some tanks change two or three times as companies merged or opted out of wagon hire. This often resulted in new owner branding and company logos.

All tank traffic offers huge modelling potential and provides countless opportunities for smaller traffic flows. Oil depots are covered in the panel opposite and as they can be found at all points on the railway network, a model depot can easily be included on a layout set anywhere in the UK (see our layout proposal, Eastoke, on page 39). Loading/unloading facilities for oil trains of various lengths usually consist of long parallel sidings at a terminal where the associated pipework and discharge valves run between the roads to enable the whole train to be emptied quickly.

Of course, modelling prototypical length block oil trains composed of 102t tankers is space hungry and might be best suited to N gauge, though an interesting example of big bogie tankers appearing in short rakes is provided by those on special traffic into Hexham yard, as illustrated on the next page.

Conceivably similar type spot traffic, for discharge into road tankers, can easily be incorporated on a layout.

For fluid and gaseous chemicals, loading and unloading facilities vary dependant upon the commodity, some might be enclosed in a shed, whilst many will be out of doors with the storage tanks and associated pipework. The Carbon Dioxide facility at Cameron Bridge is one such example dwarfed by the surrounding buildings. Of course, as we have

Modelling tank wagons

The 46t monobloc 4-wheel oil tank has been a very successful design carrying numerous Class A and Class B products. Logos, lettering and insignia have changed many times over the last thirty years depending on owners, safety regulations (eg Hazchems), refurbishment and even company cleaning policy! So for absolute authenticity in appearance for a given period it's down to personal research and studying photographs.

The Hornby 4mm model has been around for many years and is an excellent candidate for upgrading. On the above example, the walkways were lowered and ladders replaced with finer etched brass ones (D&S). Work on the underframe included; removal of incorrect moulded brake rigging, fitting brake cylinders (ABS), in-line cast brake shoes (MJT) and Oleo buffers heads (MJT). New discharge pipes and various brake linkages were knocked up from plastic tube and wire. The 15ft underframe on these models is also a good starting point for scratchbuilding other tank wagon types, such as the chlorine tank, illustrated overleaf.

102t oil tankers, but to different designs, are available in 4mm from Hornby and Lima. Detailing parts to correct items such as the bogies and buffers have been commercially available from Appleby Model Engineering.

Also in 4mm scale, several kits are available for less common tank types, such as the Carbon Dioxide vehicle from Appleby Model Engineering. A nicely completed model is illustrated in the yard of South Lancashire Transport on Mick Bryan's 00 gauge New Bryford layout.

In N gauge, Graham Farish/Bachmann offer a 102t tank model in a variety of company liveries which can be detailed further by using accessories available from Taylor Plastic Models. Peco have produced a version of the monobloc 46t tank for many years.

Top. 102t bogie tankers running in short formations are rare. Here, the remnants of Hexham goods yard in the late 1980s play host to 3 of them on a fluid chemical traffic (possibly glue). Complex loading facilities are not needed since the product is off-loaded directly into road tankers.

Far left. Thame Oil Terminal is an example of a larger rail served oil facility that would typically be suited to large layouts. 33 212 is on duty in March 1983.

Above. Another large oil terminal at Hunslet East in Leeds. Particular features here include floodlighting pylons and an intricate network of suspended safety railings. Photographed in 1994.

Left. The Albright and Wilson site at Langley Green catering for various types of chemical traffic including chlorine. Typical 'scenic' features for the modeller include pipe bridges and gantries and lots of security fencing. 31 195 is visiting in March 1985.

emphasised before, the industrial plant need not be modelled at all. The loading/unloading terminal could be as simple as a pipework manifold connected to the adjacent plant by a bulk pipeline running off scene. On a branch line, chemical traffic could well provide the reason why the route remained open. The Barton-on-Humber branch is one example of a traditional single-track line with a DMU passenger service. Up until the late '80s, it also played host to traffic of anhydrous ammonia in 88t bogie tanks running to the Britag works at Barton. Class 47s often worked the train, thus providing an opportunity to include a mainline locomotive on a branch layout. Again the concept can be used anywhere in the UK.

TTA 46T LIQUID CHLORINE TANK

Design Code TT051J TRL51649-51723

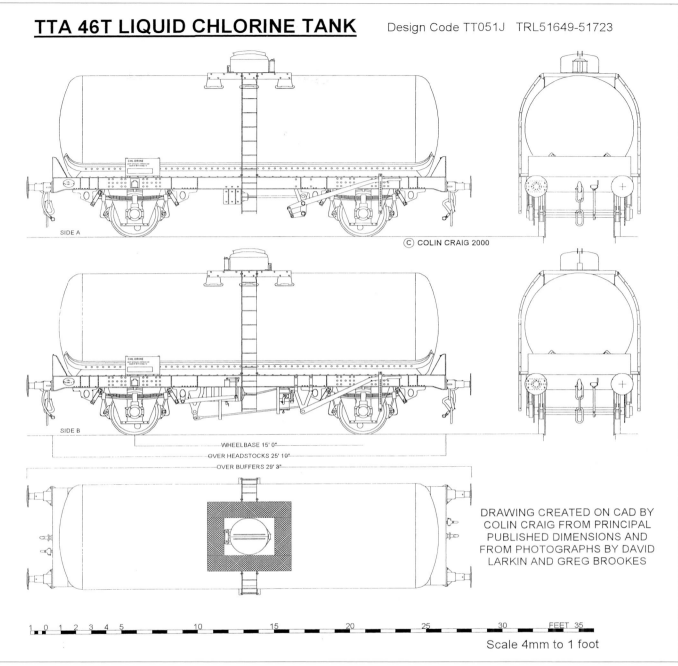

SIDE A

© COLIN CRAIG 2000

SIDE B

WHEELBASE 15' 0"
OVER HEADSTOCKS 25' 10"
OVER BUFFERS 29' 3"

CHLORINE

DRAWING CREATED ON CAD BY
COLIN CRAIG FROM PRINCIPAL
PUBLISHED DIMENSIONS AND
FROM PHOTOGRAPHS BY DAVID
LARKIN AND GREG BROOKES

1 0 1 2 3 4 5   10   15   20   25   30   FEET 35

Scale 4mm to 1 foot

NOTES: Built in 1967/8 by Charles Roberts Ltd., Horbury Junction Wakefield for Tank Rentals Ltd.

They were designed to carry liquid chlorine, hired to Associated Octel Ltd., and ICI Mond Ltd. Originally fitted with vacuum through pipe and leaf springs, in which condition they had TOPS code TTB.

Refurbishment, as shown in these drawings, saw the removal of the vacuum through pipe, the fitting of parabolic type springs and buffer over-ride plates and recoding to TTA.

These wagons are very similar to earlier builds; 1965 design code TT051Q, Nos. TRL51410 - 51430 (originally vacuum braked) and 1966 design codes TT051B/TT051M, Nos. TRL51562 - 51577. Refurbishments were similar to those on design code TT051J.

TTA Chlorine tank No TRL 51671 is pictured at Stanlow in August 1983. The lettering details on the tank show up clearly in this shot. The vehicle to the right is a BR Ferry Van being used in this train as a barrier wagon.

Cementing a Relationship

Extracted from the overall context of bulk powder traffic, cement has always been a significant rail-borne commodity. Its growth during our review period was very much a reflection of events outside the railway fence; the increase in building and road construction leading to a greatly increased demand for cement and concrete products.

Prior to the 1950s, cement, like many similar commodities, had usually been carried in bagged form in vans. However, as part of the changes to cater for the increased demand, a greater emphasis was placed on bulk transportation. This involved the major companies setting up distribution depots at strategic points throughout the country and acquiring specially designed bulk rail wagons which were increasingly utilised in block trains. Towards the end of our review, however, rail haulage of cement was on the decline, due to several factors including falling demand as well as

demise of Speedlink in 1991. However, the most noticeable aspect for the modeller are the many designs of specialised bulk cement wagon which have appeared over the review period.

Without exception, all these wagon designs have incorporated pressure discharge systems. They are thus all generically known as 'Presflos', although that name is irretrievably associated with the BR vacuum braked design made legendary amongst modellers by the Dapol (nee Airfix) kit. They were first introduced in 1954 and totalled over 2000. Although a few were utilised for other bulk powders, the vast majority have always been cement carriers. Blue Circle (otherwise known as Associated Portland Cement Manufacturers) had several hundred Presflos of their own, but as the biggest user of cement rail wagons, the firm began to develop its own designs in the early 1960s, starting with the Light Alloy (LA) or Cemflo vehicle.

In 1966 a rather different looking cement carrier appeared, the type sometimes known as the 'Chevron' or 'V' tank. The distinctive depressed centre shape was the latest measure to assist unloading and has made them possibly even better known than the Presflos. Since the rise of this design, many comparative vehicles, including some bogie stock, appeared operated by other cement companies including Tunnel, Ketton, Ribblesdale (which was later styled as Castle) and Rugby.

As with the traditional Presflo designation, all of the privately owned four-wheelers share the 'PC' group of TOPS codes, but the Chevron type is the one which is readily associated with it. Models have been produced in all three major scales, the proprietary ones in a wide range of liveries reflecting this wider usage. The 'straight tank' PCAs utilise the same wheelbase as the Chevron ones and could be a feasible conversion

Northenden Cement Terminal

Two views of the same terminal at Northenden in the Manchester area. Taken just a few years apart they show a few subtle alterations which have occurred on the site, probably due to a desire to increase capacity. The beauty with modelling a cement terminal, either large or small, is that it can be incorporated on layout set almost anywhere in the UK. Above, 47322 calls in 1989 with a selection of PCA chevron tanks, whilst, left, the depot is pictured, post-BR, in 1996.

project for the 4mm modeller whilst in N gauge they are available ready to run from Grafam Farish/Bachmann.

The non-Blue Circle PCAs were all actually examples of the growing practice of ownership by leasing companies and this sometimes led to their reassignment to other bulk powder flows. This is something that the diligent modeller of the later BR period can take particular advantage of, as there are certain credible opportunities for running formations of mixed liveries. PCAs built for cement have sometimes carried less obvious powder traffics including fly ash and mineral ores.

The above mentioned cement companies all have extensive works in many areas of the country. A full blown cement works would certainly provide interest in respect of the outgoing product as well as the various inbound raw materials, which can include coal, oil, limestone and gypsum. The sheer size of such installations however, probably puts them out of the running for most layouts, although the exchange sidings approach could be used to good effect.

A better prospect for modelling may be to consider the terminal at the user's

end of the journey, examples of which are illustrated here.

These purpose built depots vary in size, but provision of at least one storage silo is a prerequisite. Several such examples have appeared on both 4mm and 2mm exhibition layouts in recent times. Moreover, from a geographical point of view, a cement terminal is not restricted to any particular location in the UK, so such a feature is equally valid for layouts set anyway in Britain. At the minimalist extreme, for a 'spot' traffic serving a short term construction project, which could occur anywhere, the proverbial 'siding with hardstanding for pressure discharge into lorries' will do quite nicely. Despite the general prevalence of block working, both the traditional Presflo and the later PCA designs could be seen running around in small rakes throughout most of our review period, which includes the Speedlink period. Some carriage of cement products in bags and drums did occur sporadically and Blue Circle acquired a small number of long wheelbase vans suitable for pallet loading which ran into the 1970s.

Above. The cement silos at Bristol Stapleton Road depot are small enough to be adapted for use on many minimum space layouts.

Left. Demonstrating just how varied cement terminals can actually look is another 'version'. This one is sited on Ian Manderson's Easington Lane layout set in the N.E. in the mid 1970s.

Chapter Six

Layout Themes and Schemes

What if? The answer to that rather enigmatic question has probably been the basis of countless numbers of model railway layouts over the years.

It exemplifies the fictitious approach to layout building, where a might-have-been historical railway scenario is postulated to explain the *raison d'être* behind the model.

There are a precious few modellers who painstakingly recreate an actual prototype railway location, and many do it so well. Yet the vast majority of great and memorable model railways have been those which have sprung from the imagination of their builders. Borchester, Buckingham, Charmouth, Marthwaite and Winton are some of the most celebrated mid-20th century specimens which fall into this genre.

More recent, and equally creative examples in this category which focus on our chosen timescale include Hexworth, Pengwynn Crossing, Holmeworth and Carron Road.

Whilst all of these layouts portrayed fictitious localities, they undeniably exuded copious amounts of authenticity and plausibility, just the qualities that made them perpetually memorable. The point they demonstrate is, that armed with the correct historical knowledge, a good deal of imagination and a sensible application of modellers' licence, then truly convincing and realistic layouts can be conceived and built.

We have, so far, concentrated on the historical background to the British Rail era. We now apply some imagination and licence ourselves and present this small selection of our own 'just supposing' layout themes and schemes. They have all been developed using the fictional approach, a design philosophy that the authors generally favour since it allows greater freedom of creativity, something that can be restricted if modelling an actual place. Furthermore, to demonstrate that we are not just a quartet of armchair dreamers, one of them has actually been built - New Quay.

NEW QUAY (West Wales)

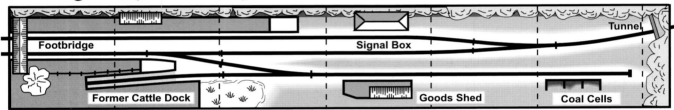

Anyone wishing to model a British Rail era location in a small space is often faced with a conundrum. Minimal layouts have traditionally been of steam branch lines, the sort of which had been mostly eradicated during the mid 1960s. After this time, branch lines often became nothing more than a long siding handling only a lonesome DMU passenger service which could make for a somewhat dull layout in terms of operation. However, all is not lost and here we outline a scheme that portrays a rural branch in the traditional mould and allows the running of a fairly varied service.

To get it all within a relatively small space, the idea borrows heavily from a minimum space scheme demonstrated by Rodney Hall in an early issue of Model Railway Journal. His pre-Grouping 'Llanastr' layout was created around the concept of building just half a station. New Quay shares this concept and portrays a Welsh outpost of the Western Region which could have provided some of the last duties for Hymeks. The actual area in which it is set is to the north west of Carmarthen where a few BR lines off the former Aberystwyth route survived until 1973 as freight only branches.

The GWR had long followed a policy of promoting and building railways to protect what it regarded as its own territory from competitors. With New Quay, the threat of a Cambrian Railway backed scheme is assumed to have spurred them into constructing a line to this resort and harbour in West Wales (not to be confused with Newquay in Cornwall).

The line continued to Aberaeron, though, beyond the tunnel, it was built as a light railway. This latter stretch now only survives

New Quay portrays the Western Region off the beaten track in West Wales. Very much a branch line theme, but one which can provide the opportunity to run Hydraulics in an authentic setting.

New Quay at a glance.

Design scale; 4mm (though equally suitable for all others).
Size of layout; 12ft x 1ft (3.65m x 0.31m) overall, scenic area 6ft 3ins x 1ft. **Period;** 1970 - 1982.
Location; West Wales (Ceredigion), on ex-GWR lines.
Locomotive classes; 35, 52, although later, 47 and 37.
Multiple unit types; Class 120.
Typical rail traffic; DMU and locomotive hauled passenger, milk (see page 86), coal with some occasional general freight.

A question of scale

Although the authors are predominantly 4mm modellers themselves, the other popular scales have not been excluded. For those already committed to a particular scale or gauge, we thus hope there will be something within these pages of relevance. On the other hand, for anyone starting out with a completely clean sheet, then adopting any of the following proposals may well be just a matter of personal taste.

Of course, it is not quite that straightforward. As hinted earlier within these pages, each of the scales offer different opportunities depending on one's particular likes and dislikes and the modelling standards adopted. Typically, we have suggested that 2mm scale/N Gauge, is probably best suited to main

line expresses and block train workings, whilst 7mm scale makes for the ideal highly detailed shunting layout. There are exceptions to all the rules of course, and equally as we can recall minimum space N Gauge branch lines, we also know of 0 Gauge block working layouts running around the garden. Sometimes it is more the modeller's resources (in terms of time, money and available space) that influences the final choice of scale, gauge and subject matter, rather than just his or her personal wishes.

The plans themselves are all drawn to scale, but each one is sized so that it best fits the page layout. However, as with every scheme in this book, each dotted grid square represents 1ft sq. (305mm x 305mm). On all the schemes too, we have avoided particularly complex pointwork

so that proprietary flexi-track and points can generally be used if preferred. However, we advise a dry run with printed point templates before committing oneself to any of the schemes - particularly those layouts which include curved pointwork.

Radical thoughts

In evolving the ideas we recognise that there isn't really anything new under the sun and the layout schemes over the following pages can all be conveniently pigeon-holed into widely used and popular configurations such as terminus to fiddle yard, continuous run, out and back, and so on. However, we have also adopted one or two more 'radical' design principles that have been successfully used in recent times. We do not claim to

The illusion of a long train is shown to good effect in this photograph and demonstrates that the 'half station' approach to layout building can be an effective weapon in overcoming the problem of lack of space.

to serve a dairy at Felin Fach. The daily goods thus winds its way from Carmarthen delivering coal and some general traffic to New Quay before the locomotive heads north to swap empty milk tanks for loaded ones.

Despite the town not having grown quite as much as the line's promoters had wished, it is assumed that there is still sufficient passenger demand to retain services. Thus, a regular Monday - Saturday DMU service is run to Swansea with holiday traffic during the summer sufficient to warrant a daily locomotive hauled train from Paddington.

However, with the length of the scenic section of the layout being no more than 6ft 3ins, the full Paddington train cannot be operated. Thus the half-station basis is used to suggest the assumed length of these trains. Only the locomotive and the front 2 coaches of the trains draw into the scenic half of the

layout. The train engine, be it a Western or a 47 then uncouples, draws forward just short of the tunnel and reverses along the up line to complete its run round manoeuvre.

The key to maintaining the illusion is of course the scenic break. The use of a wide trunk road overbridge works well in an urban environment, as does the office block straddling the station in our city scheme on page 92. However, with this country style of layout design 'stage exits' need extra careful thought. At one end the tunnel mouth provides a very conventional exit for the line north, but hiding the station is obviously much more tricky. The footbridge alone obviously can't hide the exit, so it is therefore combined with careful placing of some other 'props', such as the tree and the local bus.

The 'hardware' portrays the early 1970s with Western Region colours still very much in evidence, though by removing the goods shed and changing the station fittings, the layout could be run with stock from the early 1980s. It is assumed that the cattle dock was removed during the mid 60s to allow a greater turning area for buses.

As illustrated, the services run are those assumed for 1971. By 1976, the Hymeks would have gone and the Westerns and the milk trade would both be in their final year. Come 1981, the light railway would be disused and 47s and 37s would cover the declining holiday extras and remnant coal traffic. The one constant underscoring across all the years would be the omnipresent Class 120 Cross Country DMUs.

The scheme is decidedly simple, but is ultimately adaptable. By just changing the deciduous tree for a palm and the Crosville bus for one in Western National colours, a Devon or Cornwall location could be suggested. Furthermore, for those with interests beyond the Western Region, a line to a fictitious Lincolnshire resort around the same period could be a possibility. Obviously, ex-Great Northern fixtures and fittings would need to be added, along with Eastern Region colours, and instead of 35s and milk tanks, 31s and grain wagons would be operated. Though if it is Lincolnshire, the tunnel mouth will definitely need replacing with an alternative exit!

be the originators of the principles, but feel that they are particularly useful in enabling the many and varied aspects of British Rail to be modelled convincingly.

A principle which we have emphasised is the 'half' station concept, colloquially known as 'Bitsa Stations', the term being generally accredited to Iain Rice for his steam age schemes. Here, only half of a station is modelled, usually just one end with the main part being hidden under a suitable scenic break. For the diesel and electric period, Nigel Bowyer's Elm Park layout is a particularly memorable precursor of these designs, just within our review period.

Virtually any station with an overhead structure, be it the station building itself, an office block, a shopping centre or even a multi-storey car park, is suitable for this approach. Some well known prototype examples include Birmingham New Street, Leeds City, and Manchester Victoria. The technique is especially suited to modellers where available space is at a premium, and whilst it is instantly recognised as an ideal way to model a main line city station, the approach can also be carefully applied to smaller stations where just a footbridge exists - as is the case with New Quay.

Another approach is the multi-level layout. This is particularly suited to urban and industrial locations and provides the builder the chance to convincingly squeeze more railway into a given area. In tight spaces the theme can be taken much further with multiple exits from the scenic area into fiddle sidings and yards designed in. A particularly successful and well executed example in this genre, though just pre-dating our review period, was Walker Marine conceived by our fellow contemporary Neil Ripley.

Whatever scale and gauge is eventually adopted, the space available will probably be the final deciding factor on what format the layout will take. There are many locations around the home which can be pressed into service for use as a railway room, including spare bedrooms, attic rooms, lofts, garages, sheds and even conservatories. Certainly, some schemes are better suited as permanent layouts, but equally, some of the designs can built as portable layouts.

Freight to the forefront

Of all the themes here, there is one underlying design consideration that is featured across the board. That is, of course, the role played by railway freight activities throughout the BR era. As emphasised in previous chapters and reinforced again here, it is these varied rail freight activities which are the very essence underpinning the modelling of this period.

For some reason in the UK we have for years been stifled around modelling the old archetypal stations with their attendant goods facilities. Perhaps

Milk traffic and British Rail

Although milk had been moved by rail since the far off days when churns were collected at every country halt, it became a very low profile traffic under British Rail. It began to disappear with the onset of road competition in the 1960s, although a number of outposts held out, namely the dairies of Westmorland, including that at Appleby, and those in the better known areas of South West England and West Wales.

Wagons used on these final services were the familiar six-wheeled tank wagons that had been in service for 30 years already. Although built by a number of companies they were all broadly similar in outline and size with a capacity of about 3000 gallons and only minor design variations on tanks and underframes.

Liveries around this time tended to be plain aluminium with the colourful St Ivel white and orange scheme appearing around 1970. Milk tanks were always intended to run at speed and could be attached to passenger workings. By the early 1970s only two companies - Express Dairy and Unigate - were still using rail and traffic was by then, found only on the Western Region.

Milk from Lampeter (which inspired New Quay) saw Hymeks on some of their final duties, with 37s taking over until the end in September 1973. South West England traffic originated from St. Erth, Lostwithiel, Totnes and Torrington amongst others and the 'classic milk branch line' from Hemyock supported a flow where NB Class 22 hydraulics were used before handing over to 25s in 1971.

Most of this traffic was channelled down the Western Region Main Line to London area terminals including Vauxhall, Morden South and Kensington. Initially, Warships and Westerns were generally used with 50s and 47s in later years. The death knell sounded with the final train running in 1980 when surprisingly, the then Milk Marketing Board refurbished a fleet of 40 six-wheeled tanks and had 31 four-wheeled tanks built onto existing

West Country milk traffic in the Britiah Rail era is often associated with the NBL class 22 as seen here in the mid 1960s.

chassis. Unfortunately, very little use was made of them and after a period of storage, all bar one went for scrap, the sole survivor being acquired by the National Railway Museum.

Although confined in principle to the Western Region, the modelling of milk traffic is relatively straightforward and no special facilities are needed. Handling methods at both ends require just a siding with hardstanding or a loading dock. The product is pumped into the wagons via a flexible pipe connection whilst for unloading, discharge pipes can lead directly under adjacent platforms to the nearby creamery, as occurred at Vauxhall.

Models of six-wheeled tanks are available from Lima in 4mm in a variety of liveries (including both St. Ivel and Unigate). Slaters offer a 7mm kit, and a four-wheeled version in N gauge from Peco, could be altered to represent a six-wheeler.

ASTON GREEN

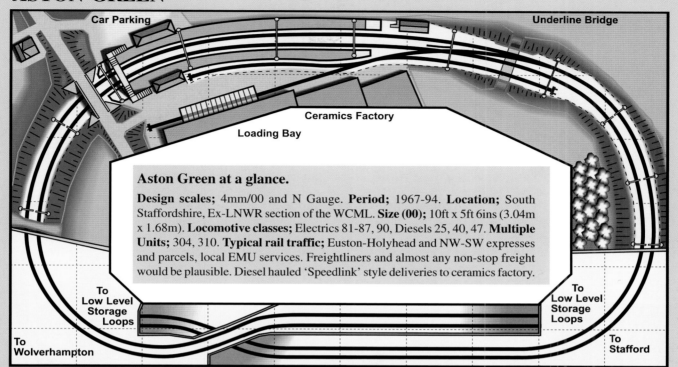

Car Parking

Underline Bridge

Ceramics Factory

Loading Bay

Aston Green at a glance.

Design scales; 4mm/00 and N Gauge. **Period;** 1967-94. **Location;** South Staffordshire, Ex-LNWR section of the WCML. **Size (00);** 10ft x 5ft 6ins (3.04m x 1.68m). **Locomotive classes;** Electrics 81-87, 90, Diesels 25, 40, 47. **Multiple Units;** 304, 310. **Typical rail traffic;** Euston-Holyhead and NW-SW expresses and parcels, local EMU services. Freightliners and almost any non-stop freight would be plausible. Diesel hauled 'Speedlink' style deliveries to ceramics factory.

To Low Level Storage Loops

To Low Level Storage Loops

To Wolverhampton

To Stafford

The 25kV lines of the LMR have long presented modellers with a dilemma. Undoubtedly a popular main line, but layouts depicting it are rare despite the availability (in 4mm) of several AC electric locomotive models. Those layouts that have appeared mostly portrayed the lines north of Crewe.

Possible reasons include the relative complexity of the Overhead Line Equipment and the lack of 25kV EMU models, essential on this section. This latter problem has recently been solved with kits for both main types now available from Southern Pride and DC Kits. To get around the OHLE problem we exploit the fact that lighter equipment was used on the less complex parts of the WCML loop from Stafford to Wolverhampton and Birmingham. This allows the use of 'look alike' catenary items from the Continental ranges. Admittedly, these may not be 100% accurate, but fastidious modellers could use them temporarily, pending the scratchbuilding of exact structures.

Though not as busy as the main Trent Valley route, this line carries a great deal of traffic and really does make for a plausible WCML layout scenario. Located between Stafford and Wolverhampton, Aston Green's surroundings reflect the pleasant rural nature of the countryside. A ceramics factory, a plausible 'lift' from the Trent Valley line, is added to give some additional operating potential. Vans collecting its wares are tripped to Wolverhampton to be fed into the Speedlink network. The only other services to be regular stoppers here are the hourly local passenger trains.

The expresses would mostly be in the hands of AC locomotives with local stoppers in the guise of class 304 and 310 EMUs. The myriad of freights passing through offer interesting opportunities for both AC locomotives and diesel traction on services heading for non-AC routes.

The small station buildings could still be the old LNW wooden ones. Only structures in urgent need of replacement were redeveloped, so original company fixtures are entirely plausible. This frugality also covered the signalling too. Despite the use of 4 aspect colour lights, an ex-LNWR signal box still controls the line.

The overbridges however, did need money spending on them to ensure adequate clearances for the OHLE. The station footbridge was replaced totally and both the road and occupation bridges sport replacement pre-cast concrete arches.

The backdrop is dominated by the ceramics factory built in functional 1950s industrial style. Other than the factory, there is only the former Station Master's house to suggest any immediate habitation, the commuter-belt village being beyond this down the lane.

As drawn, this scheme is designed with 4mm/00 gauge in mind, though is equally suited to 2mm provided the central operating well is enlarged. In the finer 4mm scales the dimensions quoted would need to be increased by a minimum of at least a metre or so all around, so as to ease the radii for EM or P4 tolerances.

Essentially an operator's layout with potential for multiple train storage, the loops of the hidden sidings being located beneath the scenic section and perhaps benefitting from some remote/automatic control.

Although requiring a room of its own, in many ways, Aston Green reinforces a key principle promoted throughout this book: Modelling the British Rail era is not restricted to unprototypical steam style branches if space is limited.

BARCONNEL JUNCTION

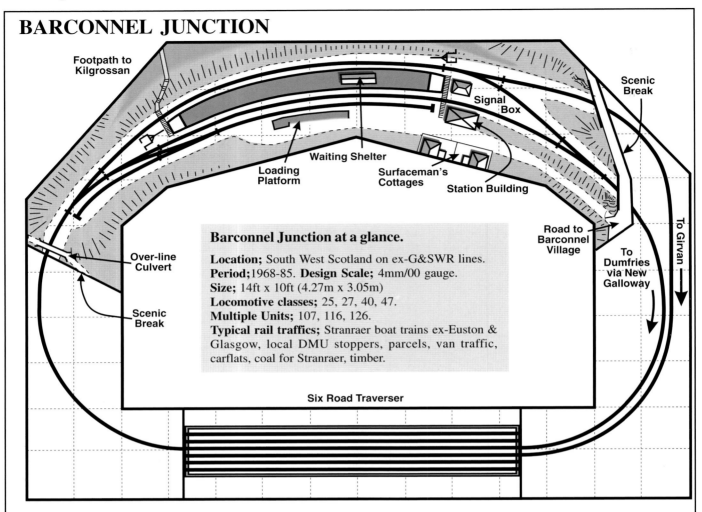

Footpath to Kilgrossan

Scenic Break

Signal Box

Waiting Shelter

Loading Platform

Surfaceman's Cottages

Station Building

Over-line Culvert

Scenic Break

Road to Barconnel Village

To Dumfries via New Galloway

To Girvan

Barconnel Junction at a glance.

Location; South West Scotland on ex-G&SWR lines.
Period; 1968-85. **Design Scale;** 4mm/00 gauge.
Size; 14ft x 10ft (4.27m x 3.05m)
Locomotive classes; 25, 27, 40, 47.
Multiple Units; 107, 116, 126.
Typical rail traffics; Stranraer boat trains ex-Euston & Glasgow, local DMU stoppers, parcels, van traffic, carflats, coal for Stranraer, timber.

Six Road Traverser

The routes of the old Glasgow and South Western are sadly often overlooked by modellers. There is definitely a special character to this railway and the men who worked it, especially the Stranraer road which is the subject of this plan. It supposes that the GSWR, tired of having to share control of the 'Port Road' (Portpatrick and Wigtownshire Rly), built a wholly owned connecting line to Stranraer from Dumfries. We've assumed that it would have gone via New Galloway and Glentrool to a point 4 miles north of Glenwhilly at Barconnel where this junction station was built.

Admittedly, modeller's licence is stretched greatly in this case, there are precious few villages, let alone towns, on our imagined route, though it would pass through the Galloway Forest providing potential for timber traffic. After closure of the Port Road, services from the south have had to take the circuitous route via Kilmarnock, not an ideal situation even though that is reality. We'll assume therefore that the two factors outlined above combined to keep this New Galloway line open.

Underlining its precarious existence, the platform at Barconnel Junction is envisaged chiefly as an interchange point. It is accessible on foot via the barrow crossing should one of the few hardy souls that inhabit the bleak moorland around this locality wish to catch a train.

Not having been much of a place to start with, the scope for rationalisation at Barconnel was thus limited and by the suggested

period, the site would appear much as it had done since the GSWR's time, save for the signs and the effects of age and weather upon the few structures still extant. This apparent time warp was not uncommon even into the mid '80s, though mostly confined to the more remote parts of the system.

Although minimal and of plain aspect, the old GSWR structures are still attractive. The signal box, which could do with a lick of paint, is of typical GSWR timber construction and is luxury compared to the miserly 'waiting shelter'.

Slightly more luxurious are the adjacent surfacemen's cottages, inhabited by Signalmen. That they reside so close to work derives from the remote location. The loading platform, once intended to cater for general goods traffic is now used to stockpile coal for the cottages and the signalbox. A lucky traveller may just glimpse the odd 16 ton mineral wagon parked up here. Other than this occasional visitor, the siding is normally home to oddments of engineering stock which lay over for considerable periods.

The stamp of the line's second owners, the LMS, is now only evident by that companies standard upper quadrant signals. British Railways' contribution was their enamelled totem signs and the attractive pale blue 'house' colours of the Scottish region which still survive here.

The tranquillity of the location is however broken frequently

BARCONNEL JUNCTION (Cont.)

by a procession of freight, parcels and passenger services on their way to and from Stranraer. Most roar through, but local DMU services stop over for a while and timber traffic from the forest reverses here en route to the Scottish papermaking factories.

Onto the layout itself and the design sets a fairly austere trackplan in the midst of moorland scenery. With few buildings and a distinct lack of trees, the plan lends itself to those who are not keen on the scenic side of modelling. Indeed, suitable representations of some buildings can obtained with a spot of kitbashing; the signalbox by adapting the Airfix/Dapol kit and the waiting shelter made from two shortened Hornby ones placed back to back.

A Traverser is suggested to cover the 'rest of the system', though pointwork could be used with equal effect. Whatever form the storage sidings take, they'll need to be able to handle class 40s and 47s plus 6 carriages to represent the longish trains which were a feature of the line. The scheme requires a spare room, attic or garage and, if you have the space, it may pay to stretch the design lengthways a little.

The combination of diesels and rugged Scottish scenery has long provided an attractive subject for modellers, quite rightly

Modelling an Inter-City class 126 DMU set for use on Barconnel Junction would be a challenging project most probably requiring scratchbuilding skills. An example is seen here at Stranraer Harbour station in 1979.

so. However, by moving to South West Scotland, you can operate longer loco hauled trains with type 4 power as well as DMU types, in particular the 126 units which were unique to the area.

understandable because of the nostalgic appeal and perception of unhurried timelessness that such locations always seem to exude. The authors agree on this, but even in the far off days before British Rail, there were many examples of railway areas where idyllic passenger stations were completely unknown. Steel works, chemical plants, MOD establishments, industrial estates and coal mine networks all fall into this category. On some routes the loss of passenger services left numerous surviving branches as freight only lines with one or more railheads and depots along the way.

We touched on some examples of these in chapter 4 and commented on the fact that American model railroaders have been successfully recreating this kind of prototype for many years now. Certainly, their minimum space switching (shunting) layouts, with several factory sidings, jetties or warehouses, all subscribe to this formula and the results, if one reads such magazines as Model Railroader can be most inspiring. Extending this modelling concept to the British scene is something that really is way overdue and the wharf scheme on page 53 reflects this.

Layouts with industrial and commercial railway terminals are undoubtedly less 'green' (in both the

political sense as well as the scenic sense!) than all those layouts portraying twee wayside stations hung-over from Edwardian times. Thus, often when modelling the BR period, those blessed plots and green and pleasant lands will have to be set aside whilst hard edged, pragmatic and environmentally un-friendly man-made constructions and carbuncles take their place.

That may sound a trifle eccentric, but then it all depends ultimately on your point of view; we would all prefer to camp amongst the daffodils, dales and woodlands, rather than adjacent to the local thermo-nuclear reprocessing plant, but in some ways the industrial juxtapositions of pipes, silos, bunkers, conveyors, storage tanks, chimneys, cranes, gantries, pits, docks, et al, all have an intangible engineering allure which often cries out to be modelled.

So, whilst the rustic and pastoral layout, branch or otherwise, can still be modelled effectively and authentically during in the BR era, further variety in layout design can be achieved if the industrial aspect is adopted. After all, the railways were invented for the conveyance of mineral commodities, the transhipment of sentimental humans from one enchanting locality to another was fairly low down the pecking order in most company prospectuses!

Some other perspectives

Another angle that is occasionally seen used on club and exhibition layouts and particularly suited to the rolling stock builder, is the multiple-period approach. Here, the modeller produces two or three sets of stock which each depict a separate historical time. The same layout is used for different operating sessions, but transformed from one period to another by the choice of locomotives and complementary stock. The net effect can almost be two, or even three, layouts for the price of one!

An extreme example might be a layout which can run an early BR period sequence with green pilot scheme diesels, maroon coaches and traditional goods stock. Next session might be the late 1970s with passenger workings provided by heritage DMU sets and surviving freight provided by one or two choice spot traffics into the goods sidings. The last session, say in the late 1980s, is then under the command of Sprinter and Pacer passenger stock with what remains of the sidings turned over to engineer's storage. Of course, such an approach needs to be tackled with care within the remit of the British Rail era. In chapter two we commented on the rapid pace of change to the railway infrastructure over the 30 year span. Rationalisation resulted in a

(Continued on page 92)

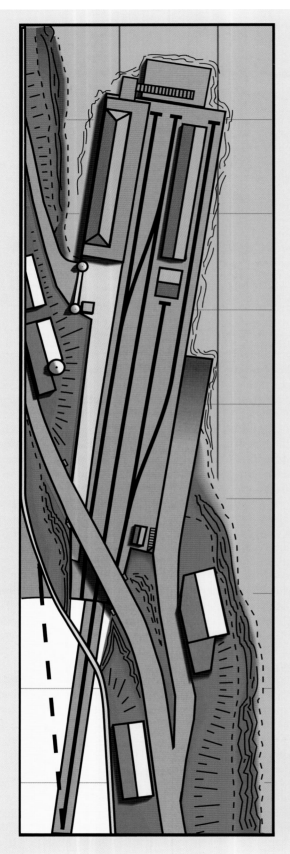

ROSHVEN

Harbour and pier scenes are popular and appealing backdrops for layouts. Trains can be set amidst romantic and picturesque fishing villages of the type which provide countless countryside calendars and chocolate box lids with scenes of red pantile roofs, tall chimney stacks and fishing smacks.

Yet, whilst dock and harbour railways were numerous, usually for shipping industrial commodities like coal and steel, the rail served fish pier was a more difficult beast to espy. This was particularly so in early diesel days when fish traffic was in decline. Nevertheless, the vision of classic diesel types shuffling box vans to and fro along a fisherman's jetty can be irresistible. Roshven was born of this irresistibility.

The real Roshven is located on the west coast of Scotland and was the original site of the proposed West Highland Extension Railway terminus from Fort William. In the event, Mallaig was chosen as the end of the line and Roshven was completely bypassed. This scheme assumes that a railway pier head serving the Inner Hebrides was actually constructed here first. The route followed the present day Mallaig line as far as Lochailort Station and then ran along the south shore of Loch Ailort to reach Roshven a further 8 miles away. Later the line to Mallaig was completed and Lochailort became the junction for the branch to Roshven.

The model portrays the location as it might have been in the late 1960s. Facilities at Roshven are sparse; the station is a small terminus built upon a pier jutting out from a rocky headland on the shore of the loch. Around the shoreline and station area are a number of small cottage dwellings making up part of this little west coast hamlet. The railway itself arrives through a steep sided cutting, emerging from under a road overbridge and onto the pier. This is of course all designed to provide a suitable scenic break between the layout and the sector plate.

The pier is of stone construction with a slipway on the seaward side and a floating pontoon for Hebridean ferries at the pier head. One railway passenger platform is provided and a timber framed station building, complete with canopy, is in situ. A little castellated arch, constructed at the station entrance adds an air of elegance to the site.

Freight facilities are equally sparse with just two sidings catering for fish traffic and light merchandise for the village, a fish shed and ice plant is located opposite the station building.

The layout itself is designed for 4mm scale with standard Peco trackwork and is entirely self contained on a 8ft 6in x 2ft 6in baseboard - ideal for the spare room. Hidden siding space is minimal, there is just room for a couple of short spurs underneath the rocky scenery at the back of the layout and reached by a single sector plate. This is quite deliberate however, as the idea is to keep the majority of stock on display most of the time. The sector plate also acts as the pointwork for the station throat and run round loop.

This is to keep the overall length as short as possible but if space permits, the length of this half of the layout could be extended and conventional pointwork installed.

Roshven offers plenty of scope for the scenic modeller with water, cliffs and a variety of different buildings as well as the opportunity to include

---

Roshven at a glance.

Design scale; 4mm/ft. 00/EM/P4. (also suitable for 2mm, 7mm & G1)
Size; 8ft x 2ft 6in (2.44m x 0.76m). **Period;** 1966 - 1970
Locomotive classes: 27, 29, (24, 25).
Typical rail traffic: The mainstay service would be the daily mixed train comprising of a brake composite (typically Mk1 BCK), parcels van, fish vans and other vacuum braked freight wagons.

COLNEBRIDGE

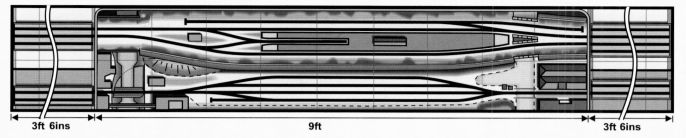

|◄ 3ft 6ins ►|◄   9ft   ►|◄ 3ft 6ins ►|

Chemical tank traffic really ought to be a more popular modelling subject since it is an aspect of rail freight which can be convincingly portrayed with short trains.

This scheme attempts to rectify the situation and utilises the fact that post-Sprinterisation, passenger train lengths generally became much reduced too.

Colnebridge is supposedly on the main trans-Pennine route via Standedge. This route is especially representative of the change to shorter train lengths, where once, type 4 classes on rakes of eight or more Mk 1s were commonplace.

To incorporate chemical traffic and create shunting interest, a split-level layout design is used. The rear half portrays an elevated station whilst the front half plays host to a shunting spur at road level providing rail access to Colnebridge's chemical plant.

The chemical commodity can be anything really, although if the aim is to be historically authentic, then careful choice of wagons appropriate for the period is essential. Furthermore, as only a few chemical tank types are available ready-to-run, the final choice of traffic may mean scratchbuilding.

Each level is independent and has separate off stage sidings which can be traversers or sector plates. The lower level includes a series of run round loops which can each handle up to four 100t type bogie tankers. Access into the chemical works is over a short bridge which crosses a canal. The freight line itself enters the scene over a road crossing which could either be ungated or have lifting barriers. The junction with the main line is assumed to be

further along the valley and hence offstage. The main lines and station sit on top of an embankment supported by heavy stone retaining walls. Only minimal facilities are now provided for passengers (another bus shelter perhaps!), which is in line with the open stations policy. The original LNWR buildings having long since been demolished.

The route once sported quadruple track but only two tracks now remain along with a refuge siding which is occasionally home to engineer's stock. An upturn in commuter traffic has seen the old bay platform reinstated and at peak times services from Leeds terminate here. Remnants of the old trackbed and the outer platforms can still be seen amidst the undergrowth. Old mill buildings are in evidence in the background.

At 16ft (4.876m) length in 4mm scale, a large spare room or garage would be needed to accommodate this scheme.

Colnebridge at a glance.

Design scale; 4mm 00/EM/P4. **Location;** West Yorkshire **Size:** 16ft x 2ft (4.876m x 0.608m). **Period;** 1988 - 1994 **Locomotive and unit types;** 47s, 37s, 142, 155, 156, 158. **Typical rail traffic;** Provincial and outer suburban passenger workings using 2nd generation unit types. Chemical tank traffic to suit personal choice but could include two or three different commodities. Also limited scope for some short through freight on main lines.

ROSHVEN (Cont)

some maritime modelling too. Although limited from an operating point of view, the scheme exploits the use of mixed trains which were still a regular turn in these parts in the 1960s and 1970s and it is envisaged that all passenger services would be in this formation. Just one coach, a couple of parcel vans, a few freight wagons and possibly some specialist fish vans would be sufficient along with two or three locomotive types. With such a small stock requirement, the layout thus lends itself for modeller to create a collection of very highly detailed models.

The scheme is suitable for N gauge and construction in the larger scales, including Gauge 1, is perfectly feasible, although bear in mind that in 0 gauge, the boards would be nearly 4ft 6in wide and 14ft in length.

A layout scheme like Roshven could also provide a plausible opportunity to run trains of short non corridor passenger stock as illustrated by this photo on the Ballachulish Branch c. 1965.

WOODHOUSE ST. GEORGES

Creating a what-if scenario for a large city station is difficult. There are countless numbers of villages on the map that were never rail connected, but there certainly aren't any city conurbations. All major cities still have at least one station, so a layout of this type requires more than just a good deal of clever imagination, it involves the invention of a might-have-been 'city' in itself. That may be stretching credibility just a bit too far, nevertheless, here goes......

Woodhouse in West Yorkshire was originally a railway town not unlike Doncaster. Throughout the 19th century it prospered as a mill town and established a red-brick university specialising in the sciences. The railway industry aspect finished with the Grouping in 1923 but Woodhouse, by now a city, developed into a thriving commercial and financial metropolis. By the late 1980s the city's through station, Woodhouse St. Georges, was a busy commuter centre with HST InterCity services to London. It also served as an axis for some trans-Pennine and NE/SW services.

Squeezing a city station into a pint pot is no mean feat, but the saving grace is again the half-station concept. London trains all terminate at St. Georges and NE/SW services have to reverse because of the routes' original alignments, thus only the locomotive/power car and the first two coaches of main line trains actually appear in the station. Locomotives loose off and run round, whilst HSTs disappear back the way they came. Through commuter services are composed of two or three car sets. Thus the maximum passenger train length need only be equivalent to three coaches, about 3ft (0.9m) in 00 gauge. Traversers are included at both ends and the overall length comes out at 15ft (4.57m). A bit large for the average spare room, but suitable for a one wall of the garage or attic. In 2mm scale the overall length would be a very manageable 7ft 6ins (2.285m).

Operationally the station is divided into up and down sides for through services whilst main line trains could technically use any platform for reversal. If space permits the left hand traverser could be replaced with sharp curves continuing the layout around the room. The front area could be developed into some low level trackwork, perhaps engineer's sidings or a wagon works.

Scenically, straddling the platforms is a goods lift, *a la* Leeds City, with a multi-storey office building immediately behind to further disguise the scenic break. High rise city buildings form the backdrop and the Woodhouse inner ring road provides the western stage exit.

Sprinter types work commuter services with surviving remnants of the 101s and 110s. 141s and 143s would be appropriate too and the odd 31 or 37 on a pair of GUVs could be justified. Main line services would be limited to HSTs and 47s on mainly Mk 2 stock.

Although track formations portray recent practice, the scheme could be back-peddled into the 1970s with traditional 2, 3 and 4 car DMUs, a wider variety of type 4 traction on main line workings and Deltics on the London trains. Equally, Woodhouse could be set in the electric age with class 91s, and 25kV 308s in WYPTE livery as well as the ubiquitous 156 and 158s. Although not a tail-chasing style of layout, it does provide yet another opportunity for fine detail modelling.

Woodhouse St. Georges at a glance.

Design scale; 4mm 00/EM/P4. Also suitable for N gauge.
Location; West Yorkshire. **Size;** 15ft x 2ft 9in (4.57m x 0.838m). **Period:** 1988-1992. **Locomotive classes;** 47, HST.
Multiple Units; 101, 110, 142, 155, 156, 158.
Typical rail traffic: All passenger, through trans-Pennine services plus main line London trains and NE/SW services. Some scope for parcel working and engineer's trains.

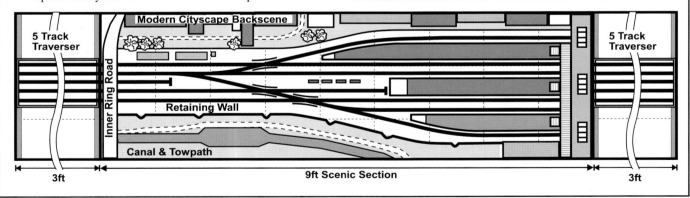

multitude of irreversible transformations that could make the multi-period approach difficult to achieve. Like, for example, the trimming back of terminus stations such as Windermere, Saltburn, St Ives and Blackpool South, or major station rebuilds such as Waverley, Crewe and York. All these localities by 1994 were far, far different to what they had been in 1964. That said, choosing a specific threshold of change, when either

new passenger stock or new freight stock appeared almost overnight, could allow a dual period concept to be tackled with just a matter of weeks between the two phases.

Maximising believability

A philosophy and goal that preoccupies and drives many within this delightful hobby is the need to achieve 'believability' in their modelling.

Believability is that sought after quality in a model which oozes with authenticity and plausibility. It possesses the power to engage the observer in a state of undiverted reverie, whisking them away to the very time and place which the layout depicts.

Believability does mean different things to different people of course. To some, only ultimate scale accuracy can create the illusion, for others it takes a

WALLINGFORD ROAD

If British Rail was to be credited with just one outstanding success, it must surely have been the High Speed Train. Even today, 24 years after their introduction, they are still impressive to watch as they roar by.

However, even a 2+7 formation takes up some 8ft 6in (2.6m) in 4mm scale. In N gauge this becomes manageable at 4ft 3in (1.3km) and the potential to replicate a stretch of main line large enough to take a HST in full flight exists within the confines of an average domestic garage. The plan is an abstract version of Cholsey and Moulsford on the Western Region Main Line. Unlike most other wayside stations between Paddington and Didcot, Cholsey retained all its platforms, though only the relief line ones are officially in use. Also the GWR station architecture survived beyond the demise of steam and our version follows suit.

Wallingford Road purports to be the original station provided to serve the locality prior to the opening of the Wallingford branch 1868. In this miniature world, the branch to Wallingford has also been kept open for passenger as well as grain traffic. The mainstay of the passenger traffic on the main lines are the HSTs supplemented by locomotive hauled expresses, such as the Hereford/Worcester and Oxford services which had class 50s in charge of them until the late '80s. Also 47s could be seen on cross country services which came off the Oxford line heading for the Southern Region via Reading. Class 117 DMUs round off the picture on stopping trains and the branch is home to the ubiquitous 'bubble' car.

Parcels duties were shared between 31s and 47s, although the West of England TPO was often a class 50 turn. A one time consequence of HST operations was the need to send express parcels separately due to the limited size of the guard's compartments in power cars. Thus a Class 31 could oft be seen scurrying flat out along the main line with just a GUV or two in tow.

Freight traffic is mostly block working; aggregates from the Mendips, Freightliners to and from Southampton and the North, and oil tankers bound for various terminals. Speedlink services also used the line and the supposed grain traffic on the branch would have required a trip working.

From 1992, the Thames Turbo classes, 165 and 166, gradually took over on secondary services and after mid '93, the only locomotive hauled passenger trains were those of InterCity's Cross Country sub-Sector.

At the start of our suggested timescale, 31s, 37s and 47s did almost all of the freight work. Slowly, types 5s were drafted onto the heavier services and by the 1990s, 56s, 59s and 60s were as common as the old stalwarts.

In model form the bulk of the stock is available courtesy of Graham Farish/Bachmann whilst many of those which are not available R-T-R can be acquired in kit form.

As drawn, the scheme is almost two layouts in one, as there is no connection between the main or relief lines, though this could be added in the hidden section if desirable. The main lines could be wired for automatic operation with relief lines wired for manual as well. Thus, when a break from operating is due, you just throw the switch to auto, sit back with a cuppa, and watch the trains go by..............

Wallingford Road at a glance.

Design Scale; 2mm/N gauge (only really suitable for this scale).   **Period;** 1980-1994.
Location; South Oxfordshire, Ex-GWR.   **Size of layout;** 19ft x 3ft 6in (5.8m x 1.07m).
Locomotive classes; 31, 37, 47, 50, 56, 59, 60, HSTs. **Multiple units;** 117, 121, 165, 166.
Typical rail traffic; Paddington to Bristol and South Wales expresses, local DMU services to Oxford, N/S cross country services. Parcels and TPO, Freightliners, aggregates and oil block workings, speedlink trips and through workings.

fully landscaped vista to transport them off to their absolute arcadia. Whilst a degree of compromise in scale accuracy is often tolerated, what can destroy believability with great fervour are those hopeless gaffs in the historical or geographical aspects of the layout.

At one extreme, running a Deltic on a WCML express, would be inexcusable. A lesser mistake, such as using the wrong wagons for a given period and location may not appear quite so bad but, fundamentally, as with life in general, most of us want to do things as correctly as possible and creating a model railway, whether for exhibition or private use, is no exception. There will still be, if the fancy takes them, those modellers who'll happily close their railway room door and operate their LMS Duchess alongside their APT whilst telling us politely to mind our own business. But, in the final analysis, we do feel that there are many who share the philosophy that the greatest fulfilment in this hobby occurs when everything on the layout is as believable as possible.

Above all else, a believable, authentic and plausible model railway will succeed in '*taking you there*'.

Table 1. Locomotive Lifelines - The Main Line Diesels

Years in Service (64–94). Approximate service spans by class:

Class	Years in Service
15v	64–71
16v	64–68
17v	64–71
20	64–94
21v	64–68
22v	64–71
23v	64–71
24v	64–80
25	64–87
26	64–92
27	64–87
28v	64–68
29v	64–71
31	64–94
33	64–94
35v	64–75
37	64–94
40	64–85
41v	64–67
42v	64–72
43v	64–71
44v	64–80
45	64–88
46	64–84
47	64–94
50	66–92
52	64–78
53	64–75
55	64–81
56a	76–94
58a	82–94
59a	90–94
60a	90–94

v - All examples of the class were vacuum braked only. **a** - All examples of the class were air braked only.   Refer to Platform 5 and/or Ian Allan guides for braking details of specific locomotives.

Appendix 1. - Modern Train Description Headcodes

Throughout railway history various systems of train description have been used for the benefit of signalling and operating staff. Examples include the familiar headlamp codes used on the leading end of locomotives to denote the class of train, the Southern Region's own two-digit alpha-numeric roller blind codes signifying routes and similar two-character codes originally intended for use on DMU services.

Early in the 1960s a four-character train description system became standard on most of British Railways. This is the definitive system for the modeller of the British Rail era and the codes themselves are still used today to identify trains to signalmen and describe them in working timetables. From about 1959, all new motive power was fitted with a system of roller blind displays in place of the old four disc/ lamp system. These became colloquially known as the 'Headcode Boxes'.

Of the actual codes (e.g. 1A02) displayed by locomotives throughout the '60s and early '70s, the first numerical character signifies the class of train, based on a descending order of speed and importance, the second character, a letter, relates to the train's destination, the last two numerical characters are either an individual train number or a route number.

A listing of actual codes used would be a huge undertaking and of course, unless a model locomotive is fitted with some very intricate miniature roller blind mechanism or sub-miniature electronic display, it cannot be modelled with the correct code all the time! However, from January 1976 there was no longer a requirement to display the four-character codes on trains. For about 18 months locomotives could be seen running with a 0000 code until about 1978 when the use of two white discs became almost universal. Commencing from about 1980, headcode boxes began to be either plated over or removed and locomotives were fitted with various permutations of marker lights and headlamps.

Table 2. DMUs - The TOPS Coded 1st Generation.

Class	Builder	Type	Formations as intro.	Regional Allocations 1964	Regional Allocations 1978	Regional Allocations 1991	W/drawn by	G	B	W	BG	N	R	Se
100	Glo'ster RCW	G/P	2 car	Sc, LM	LM, E	-	1984	X	X					
101	Metro - Cam.	G/P	2, 3, 4 car	Sc, LM, NE	Sc, LM, E, W	NSE, RR, Sct	2000+	X	X	X	X	X	X	X
103	Park Royal	G/P	2 car	LM	LM	-	1983	X	X					
104	B'ham RCW	G/P	2, 3, 4 car	LM, NE	LM, E	NSE, RR	1992	X	X		X*	X		
105	Cravens	G/P	2, 3 car	LM, NE, E	LM, E	-	1988	X	X		X*			
107	BR Derby	G/P	3 car	Sc	Sc	Sct	1992	X	X		X			X
108	BR Derby	G/P	2, 3, 4 car	LM, NE	LM, E	RR, NSE	1993	X	X	X	X	X		
109	Wickham	G/P	2 car	E	-	-	1971	X	X					
110	B'ham RCW	G/P	3 car	NE	E	RR	1992	X	X	X	X			
111	Metro - Cam.	G/P	2, 3, 4 car	NE	E	-	1989	X	X	X	X			
112	Cravens	G/P	2 car	LM	-	-	1969	X	X					
113	Cravens	G/P	2 car	LM	-	-	1969	X	X					
114	BR Derby	G/P	2 car	E	E	RR	1992	X	X	X	X			
115	BR Derby	Sub.	4 car	LM	LM	NSE	1992	X	X	X	X	X		
116	BR Derby	Sub.	3 car	W, LM	W, LM, Sc, E	RR	1994	X	X	X	X			
117	Pressed Steel	Sub.	3 car	W	W	NSE	2000+	X	X	X	X	X	X	
118	B'ham RCW	Sub.	2, 3 car	W	W	RR, NSE	1995	X	X		X	X		
119	Glo'ster RCW	C.C.	3 car	W, LM	W, LM	RR, NSE	1995	X	X		X	X		
120	BR Swindon	C.C	2, 3 car	W, Sc	W, LM, Sc	-	1990	X	X		X			
121	Pressed Steel	Sub.	1, 2 car	W	W	RR, NSE	1999	X	X	X	X	X	X	
122	Glo'ster RCW	Sub.	1, 2 car	W	W, LM, Sc	RR	1994	X	X		X		X	
123	BR Swindon	I/C	4 car	W	E	-	1984	X	X		X			
124	BR Swindon	I/C	6 car	NE	E	-	1984	X	X		X			
125	BR Derby	Sub.	3 car	E	-	-	1977	X	X					
126	BR Swindon	I/C	3, 6 car	Sc	Sc	-	1982	X	X		X			
127	BR Derby	Sub.	4 car	LM	LM	-	1984	X	X					

Regional/Sector Codes: E = Eastern Reg., NE = North Eastern Reg., W = Western Reg., LM = London Midland Reg., Sc = Scottish Reg., NSE = Network Southeast, RR = Regional Railways, Sct = Scotrail.
Livery Notes: G = Green, B = plain Rail Blue, W = White/Blue stripe, BG = Rail Blue and Grey, N = Network Southeast, R = Regional Railways, Se = Strathclyde. Those denoted with an asterisk (*) indicate that only a few examples carried the livery.
Formations quoted were as built, except classes 125, 126, 127, they were all of 'blue' square coupling code and could technically be run together in mixed formations.

Table 3. DMUs - The Second Generation, Production Series

Class	Builder	Cars/unit	Introduced	Intended use	Sectors/common locations of use pre-1994
141	BREL/Leyland	2	1984	Commuter/Secondary	Provincial - WYPTE area services only.
142	BREL/Leyland	2	1985	Commuter/Secondary	Provincial - Mainly North of England (exc. 'Skippers').
143	Barclay/Alexander	2	1985	Commuter/Secondary	Provincial - Mainly North of England.
144	BREL/Leyland	2/3	1986	Commuter/Secondary	Provincial - Mainly North of England WYPTE services.
150/1	BREL	2*	1985	Cross Country/Secondary	Provincial - Wales, Midland/ Northern/ Eastern Ctys.
150/2	BREL	2*	1986	Cross Country/Secondary	Provincial - Wales, Midland/ Northern/ Eastern Ctys.
153	Leyland	1	1991	Secondary/Branch	Provincial - Most areas except Scotland and South.
155	Leyland	2	1987	Cross Country***	Provincial - Now only WYPTE services.
156	Metro-Cammell	2**	1987	Cross Country/Expresses	Scotrail/Provincial - All areas except South and West.
158	BREL	2/3	1990	Cross Country/Expresses	Scotrail/Provincial - All areas except South and West.
159	BREL	3	1993	Cross Country/Expresses	NSE - Mainly West of England express routes.
165/0	BREL	2	1991	Cross Country/Secondary	NSE - Mainly Chiltern area routes.
165/1	BREL	2/3	1992	Cross Country/Secondary	NSE - Mainly Thames corridor commuter routes.
166	BREL	3	1993	Cross Country/Expresses	NSE - Mainly Thames corridor express routes.

* Units have run as 3 car sets using split 150/2 sets as centre cars. ** Units have run as 3 car sets using split sets as centre cars. *** All except 10 WYPTE sets were converted to 153s in 1991-93. All dates show 'official' service entry dates, plus original intended duties.

Appendix 2. - The Use of Brakevans.

One of the criteria affecting the correct formation of freight trains in our review period is the simultaneous operation of unfitted, vacuum-braked and air-braked freight vehicles.

This complicated mix of braking systems is something which is characteristic to the BR era, and for the modeller, it manifests itself in a number of ways. First perhaps, is the automatic brake equipment which includes such aspects as the type and position on vehicles of cylinders, tanks, rigging, levers, lettering, etc. This is very relevant to wagon modelling aficionados, but is too huge a topic to cover here. The correct use of a brakevan, however, is a very visual aspect of layout operation and can be covered with this basic 'bluffer's guide'.

From the earliest times, freight trains were provided with at least one brakevan on all but short distance workings along goods only lines. In 1968 an agreement with the trade unions allowed the guard of a continuously braked freight train (with *either* a vacuum *or* an air system) to travel in the rear cab of the locomotive. This reduced the need for brakevan stock at a stroke, although they were still required on trains which were marshalled of vehicles with incompatible braking systems; e.g. if unfitted and fitted vehicles (vacuum or air) were in the consist, or a complete train of air braked wagons had to be hauled by a locomotive without such equipment (such as steam engines, or those diesels that were never fitted with it - see table 1). Similarly, a train might include both vacuum and air braked vehicles, but as only one system can be activated at a time by the locomotive (and only if the appropriate stock is marshalled together next to it), then a brakevan would be required. Some flexibility is provided by vehicles which are 'through piped', although these would still need a quantity of vehicles fitted with the operable braking system at the rear of them.

One situation which could not be worked after the 1968 agreement was when a fitted train was hauled by a diesel with only one cab - either a shunter or Type 1. When working solo a brakevan was thus still necessary and even when they worked in pairs, the guard still had no independent control of the train brakes until the mid '80s when many class 20s were fitted with an additional valve. However, concurrent with all this was the spread of Driver Only Operation (DOO) which eventually covered most fully fitted freights by the late '80s.

The handrails of a brakevan can just be seen behind the large air braked bogie van on this short train from Cowley Goods Depot c.1980. A brakevan is required as one or other of the braking systems in the consist will be inoperable.

Certain categories of fitted trains also provided noteworthy exceptions, principally those conveying hazardous cargoes and thus also requiring the provision of barrier wagons. Other special cases in which brakevans were retained involved certain local propelling movements (see pages 39 and 76) and on freight only branches where the train crew were responsible for opening and closing minor level crossing gates.

This whole state of affairs lasted a long time due to the protracted implementation of air braking. Even in the 1980s some 31s and 37s, for instance, still had only vacuum train brakes.

If all this sounds complicated, well, it is! It is perhaps a safe bet to hang a brakevan onto any train which includes stock of traditional outline, and before DOO, even air braked trip workings might convey one for any of the reasons above. As for the vehicle itself, the safest catch-all for the diffident modeller is a bauxite liveried BR standard, a long lived type which can be considered appropriate for just about every situation.

Appendix 3. - Bibliography.

A Pictorial Record of British Diesel Multiple Units.
Brian Golding. Cheona Publications.
Modelling Diesels in 4mm Scale.
Tim Shackleton. Hawkshill Publications.
Modelling BR Today.
Chris Leigh. Ian Allan.
Thoroughly Modern Models 1. Diesels in 4mm.
Thoroughly Modern Models 2. Modern Wagons in 4mm.
Both Nigel Burkin. Irwell Press.
Working Wagons Volume 1 1968 - 1973.
Working Wagons Volume 2 1974 - 1979.
Both David Larkin. Santona Publications.
Railways in Profile Series.
Geoff Gamble. Cheona Publications.
British Main Line Diesel Locomotives
Marsden and Fenn. OPC/Ian Allan.
British Railfreight - Today and Tomorrow.
Geoffrey Freeman Allan. Janes/Ian Allan.
An Illustrated History of BR Wagons.
Bartlett, Larkin, Mann, Silsbury, Ward. OPC.

Modern Private Owner Wagons on British Rail.
David Ratcliffe. OPC.
British Railways Wagons, The First Half Million.
Don Rowland. David and Charles.
Freight Only Volumes. 1, 2 and 3.
M Rhodes and P Shannon. Silverlink Publications.
BR Fleet Survey (Booklet series).
Brian Haresnape. Ian Allan.
British Railway Mk 1 Coaches.
Keith Parkin. HMRS/Pendragon.
BR Mk 2 Coaches.
Michael Harris.
An Illustrated History of West Country China Clay Trains
John Vaughan. OPC.

Useful reference and inspiration can be gleaned from the numerous picture albums from publishers such as OPC, Ian Allan, Bradford Barton, etc. Of particular interest, despite much of the material being pre-1964, is 'Scottish Urban and Rural Branch Lines' by George C. O'Hara, published by Eroxop Ltd.

For numbering and technical details of specific locomotives, multiple units and coaches the Platform 5 and Ian Allan series of combined volumes are invaluable.